Ten Principles with Promise

Ten Principles with Promise:

The Parable of the Swing Set

by

Lindon J. Robison

Published and distributed by:

Granite Publishing and Distribution, LLC
868 North 1430 West
Orem, Utah 84057
(801) 229-9023 • Toll Free (800) 574-5779
Fax (801) 229-1924

Page Layout & Design by Myrna Varga, The Office Connection, Inc.
Cover Design by Tamara Ingram
Edited by: James D. Smith & Lana Bailey

ISBN: 1-932280-84-7
Library of Congress Control Number: 2005925522

Printed in the United States of America
FC Printing, Salt Lake City, UT
1 3 5 7 9 10 8 4 6 4 2

Acknowledgments

꧁

My wife Bonnie and children, Ryan, Lana, Rachel, Adam, and Nathan, made significant contributions to the writing of this book. Ryan's Eagle scout project provided the sub title for this book, *The Parable of the Swing Set*. Lana and Rachel edited different drafts and presented them to me as Father's Day and Christmas presents. Adam suggested eliminating two chapters, a decision that shortened the text and focused the message. Nathan encouraged me to keep trying to get it right. Finally, my life with my wife Bonnie has given me something to write about. She is my best friend and partner in learning about and trying to live correct principles.

Others also made important contributions to this book. Michele Steed suggested ways to improve the clarity and organization of the entire book. Her suggestions for changing chapter one on the nature of principles were particularly helpful. Richard Winder has been a continual source of new ideas and insights. Daniel Judd first taught me about the importance of balance and warned against the alternatives to repentance. Wendy Bromley made the helpful comparison between writing and art. She taught me that great books and great paintings practice repetition with variation. Gloria Lowry suggested ways to improve the presentation of several important topics covered in this book. Later in the writing of this book, two Brethren of the Seventy, Hyde and Roxanne Merrill, Leslie Randle,

George Owen, and Jean Blake read the entire text, corrected mistakes, checked references, and made helpful suggestions.

A condensed version of the last chapter was published in the *Ensign* magazine. I appreciate their permission to publish the expanded version of that article in this book. Finally, I thank all those who have helped bring this book to print and especially for friends and family who have taught me gospel principles by demonstrating them in their daily walk.

With kind regards,

Lindon J. Robison
July 2005

Contents

✦

Introduction

❧

The Lord revealed to the Prophet Joseph Smith that Zion could only be established among the Saints when they followed correct principles practiced in the celestial kingdom (D&C 105:5). So, Joseph Smith made the teaching of correct principles his priority. When once asked how he governed his people, he responded: "I teach them correct principles and they govern themselves."[1]

The need for correct principles. Several years ago on a summer's day, my family and I left our comfortable Michigan home to spend a sabbatical year at Brigham Young University. We had prepared carefully for our trip, packing those things that we believed were necessary for our stay into a U-haul trailer to be pulled by one of our seasoned "horses," a dependable Dodge Aspen station wagon.

During the first day of our trip through Michigan and Illinois, our dependable Dodge delivered mile after mile of reliable service. However, as evening approached, our car began to lose power until, finally, it could barely climb even small hills. At last we were forced to rest our exhausted horses at the nearest motel. The motel clerk told us about a garage a few miles away where we might find help. So, the next morning we limped to the mechanical aid station. The mechanic there diagnosed our car's problem as a lack of engine pressure and prescribed a newer engine. We considered our options: abandon our formerly dependable Dodge and buy another car, or replace the engine—a less expensive option. Frugality won out and we agreed to the engine replacement.

For the next two and a half days while our car was being repaired, my family and I hung out in the Tipton Iowa city park. The days we spent in Tipton were the hottest on record for that time of year, and some of our children claimed they could hear the corn wilt! Finally the mechanic completed the engine replacement and invited me to test drive my mechanically altered Aspen. Hopefully I slid behind the steering wheel and stepped on the gas. I expected a powerful leap. Instead, my Dodge yawned, just as before. I sat there shocked and disappointed. I believed I had done everything possible to restore my car's former vigor. What more could I do?

The mechanic re-evaluated his work. "Perhaps," he mused, "the problem wasn't the engine but a plugged catalytic converter." His second diagnosis was correct. The mechanic had replaced a healthy engine. Had he diagnosed my car's problem correctly in the first place, my car's mechanical problem could have been solved quickly and relatively inexpensively. Furthermore, after replacing my healthy engine, the plugged catalytic converter still had to be fixed.

Sometimes at family gatherings, and always on our trips through Iowa, my family and I review our engine replacement experience. Besides teaching me to get a second opinion when considering major car repairs, this incident taught our family an invaluable lesson regarding incorrect beliefs and their consequences. The lesson we learned was that our actions are determined by our beliefs about how best to satisfy our needs. If our beliefs are correct, then our actions will likely produce successful outcomes. However, if our beliefs are incorrect, then our actions are unlikely to produce successful outcomes no matter the amount of our effort we expend attempting to satisfy our needs.

The consequences of a mistaken engine diagnosis are minor compared with the consequences of other mistaken beliefs. Blood letting was a sometimes fatal medical procedure resulting from mistaken beliefs about diseases. The *Titanic* sank because the ship's officers lacked essential navigational information. Ford Motor Company introduced the Edsel car because their market analysts held mistaken beliefs about consumer demands.

Incorrect beliefs about man's relationship to God have led to human sacrifices among ancient Indian cultures, the Huguenot massacre in France, pogroms in Russia, slavery in America, the Holocaust in Europe, years of terror in Northern Ireland, ethnic cleansing in Bosnia and Kosovo, and religious wars in Afghanistan, Iran, and Iraq. Incorrect beliefs about the creation and Adam and Eve's relationship to God have for centuries contributed to the mistreatment of women. The false belief that there is no God, and therefore no right or wrong, has led many to pursue their selfish lusts without concern for others. Finally, the mistaken belief that profits are more important than people has led some producers to sell harmful substances including alcohol, tobacco, illegal drugs, and unhealthy foods.

To avoid the evils of the world just described, we need correct information about man's relationship to God. We need correct principles. But where can we find such information?

One time in our stake, a Christian minister was invited to speak to an institute class of our young adults. The minister emphasized the puniness of man's understanding compared to God's. He continued by saying that man, with his limited knowledge, could never understand the nature of God. Then a student asked: "But couldn't God reveal Himself to man?" The minister responded: "Oh, I suppose He could, but He wouldn't."

The great tragedy is that so many share this minister's mistaken view that God is unwilling or unable to reveal Himself and correct principles to man today as He did in days past. The correct answer to the student's question is that God has revealed Himself and correct principles to prophets in the past, does so today, and will continue to do so in the future. Abraham, Moses, Isaiah, and Jacob in ancient times and Joseph Smith and Gordon B. Hinckley in modern times have received revelations from God, including important information about God's work and glory—which is the exaltation, eternal life, and happiness of man. Our task is to learn from the prophets correct principles so we can govern ourselves. But first, we must answer the question: what is a principle?

Preface

Principles

∽

I once listened to an inspired sacrament meeting speaker quote Joseph Smith: "I teach them correct principles and they govern themselves." I wondered to myself, what is a gospel principle? I could catalogue gospel guidelines such as, "pay your tithing" and "live the golden rule." But I wasn't sure if these were principles.

I turned to the *Topical Guide* in my scriptures and looked up the word *principle*. There I found references to "a principle with promise," "first principles," and learned that the power of the priesthood cannot be handled or controlled only upon the "principle of righteousness." Later I read a general conference talk delivered by President Boyd K. Packer in which he defined a principle as: "an enduring truth, a law, a rule you can adopt to guide you in making decisions. Generally, principles are not spelled out in detail. That leaves you free to find your way with an enduring truth, a principle, as your anchor."[1]

After reading President Packer's talk I thought, *of course*! Principles are enduring or first truths that exist independent of man's effort to change or enforce them. But I wondered, are there different kinds of truths and therefore different kinds of principles?

There are at least three kinds of principles: principles that describe, principles that define, and principles that connect outcomes to past, present, and future actions. It is this third kind of principle that is sometimes referred to as a "principle with promise" and will be the focus of this book.

Principles that describe. Principles that describe provide details about persons, places, things, and ideas. Sometimes words that describe and words being described are connected by words like *has* and *have.* An example of a principle that describes is: "the Father and the Son have bodies of flesh and bones as tangible as man's." Recently, Elder John B. Dickson of the Seventy provided several other examples of principles that describe. These include: God has a plan of happiness for the human family; Jesus Christ organized His church during His mortal ministry; the gospel of Jesus Christ has been restored; missionaries have been called of God to teach the gospel; and mankind can know with assurance that the gospel is true.[2]

Principles That Define

Principles that define, equate words or groups of words using connectors like *is* and *are.* Let *A* and *B* represent expressions of meaning. A defining principle may take the form "*A is B.*" Defining principles can be very useful, especially when we wish to know more about *A* using information we already know about *B.*

Some examples of defining principles include: faith *is* the assurance of things hoped for and the evidence of things not seen; charity *is* the pure love of Christ; and God's work and glory *is* to bring to pass the immortality, eternal life, and happiness of man.

A special kind of defining principle is an ethical statement that defines good and evil. For example, after the creation of Adam, God declared that "it *is* not good for man to be alone" (Genesis 2:18). To His detractors, the Savior posed the ethical question: "*Is* it lawful on Sabbath days to do good, or to do evil? To save life, or to destroy it?" (Luke 6:9). Finally, Alma defined good and evil when he taught that good *is* that which cometh from God and evil *is* that which cometh from the devil (Alma 5:40).

Principles with Promise

Principles that define or describe are the foundations for principles with promise that connect actions and outcomes, and commandments and blessings. Alma explained: "Therefore God gave unto them commandments, after having made known unto them the plan of redemption, that they should not do evil" (Alma 12:32). Teaching those defining and describing principles contained in the plan of redemption gave meaning to the commandments that followed.

Principles with promise that connect actions and outcomes often begin with a commandment from the Lord *A* followed by the promised blessing *B*. Principles with promise that connect past actions with their outcomes may take the form: *because A then B*. Principles that describe outcomes conditional on current or future choices may take the form: *if A then B* or *when A then B*.[3]

One principle that connects future outcomes to a past action declares: *Because* of the Atonement of Jesus Christ [*then*] all mankind may be saved. Another principle that connects future outcomes to our current choices promises: *If* we honor our father and mother, *then* our days upon the earth will be lengthened.

The Word of Wisdom is a principle with promise (D&C 89:3, 11). The principle is that *if* we will follow the Lord's diet with prudence and thanksgiving, *then* we will enjoy improved health and shall find wisdom and great treasures of knowledge and shall run and not be weary and shall walk and not faint. God, who desires that we enjoy good health and hidden treasures of knowledge, commands us to control what we include in our diets. Another principle with a promise is: *if* we retire and arise early, *then* we will not be weary and our bodies and minds will be invigorated (D&C 88:124). God, who desires us to enjoy the blessing of an invigorated mind and body, directs us to retire and arise early.

Understanding principles also helps us to understand the important difference between sin and mistakes. When we know the principle and "doeth it not, to him it is sin" (James 4:17). When we sin, we are commanded to repent and return to the correct principle (Ezekiel 33:15). In contrast to a sin is a mistake or an error. We err when we choose an improper action because we don't know the principle or because we lack the skill required to complete the correct action. When we err, we must learn the correct principle (D&C 1:24–26).

Patriarchal blessings often provide personalized principles. Harold B. Lee once recalled listening to a Sunday School lesson taught by the son of a patriarch. The son said he used to write down the blessings of his father and noticed that his father gave what he called "iffy" blessings. He would give a blessing, but it was predicated on "if you will not do this" of "if you will cease doing that." The son continued: "I watched these men to whom my father gave the 'iffy' blessings, and I saw that many of them did not heed the warning that my father as a patriarch had given, and the blessings were never received because they did not comply."[4]

Sometimes the Lord directs an action without describing the outcome to follow. Examples of commands that do not specify an outcome include: thou shalt not lie; thou shalt not steal; and thou shalt not covet. Obedience to God's commands without knowing the outcomes requires that we exercise our faith in the principle that our obedience to God's commandments will produce blessings. Because all of God's commandments are embedded in principles that produce blessings for those who obey, we sometimes refer to commandments as "principles." Thus the commandments to be honest and chaste may be called the principle of honesty and the principle of chastity.

Elder Dallin H. Oaks described an event in the life of his grandmother that illustrates the importance of obedience to God's command even though the outcome has not been carefully described. Elder Oaks writes:

> As a young girl, my grandmother, Chasty Olsen Harris . . . was tending some children who were playing in a dry riverbed near their home in Castle Dale, Utah. Suddenly she heard a voice that called her by name and directed her to get the children out of the riverbed and up on the bank. It was a clear day, and there was no sign of rain. She saw no reason to heed the voice and continued to play. The voice spoke to her again, urgently. This time she heeded the warning. Quickly gathering the children, she made a run for the bank. Just as they reached it, an enormous wall of water, originating with a cloudburst in the mountains many miles away, swept down the canyon and roared across where the children had played. Except for this impelling [and directing] revelation, she and the children would have been lost.[5]

Principles and Rules

There is a difference between rules and principles. The religious rulers of Christ's time taught rules. Christ taught principles. Rules direct specific actions and limit our choices. Principles point us to desired outcomes but allow us the freedom to choose the path to our goal. Rules are not universally applicable because they lack flexibility. Principles are universally applicable because they encourage the exercise of agency to adjust to unique circumstances. Rules focus on dos and don'ts. Principles emphasize possibilities. We are to be governed by principles instead of rules because rules may get in the way of each other, as the following incident demonstrates.

A mother and father established a rule for the evening behavior of their children. The rule was that after the children had said their evening prayers and had their request for a drink of water met, they could not get out of bed until morning. After one particularly trying day, and with the children finally tucked in bed, the mother was relaxing in the kitchen with a cookie and a glass of milk. Then she heard the patter of little feet and saw her three small children approaching. In a somewhat irritated voice she called to her husband, "do we make an exception or do we enforce the rule?" To her surprise, the youngest child, replied: "keep the rule mommy." Wondering if the small child really understood the rule she asked: "and what's the rule?" The young daughter promptly replied: "always share."[6]

Another example of rules getting in the way of those wanting to practice correct principles involved Mother Teresa. Mother Teresa and her Nuns of Charity one time wanted to renovate an abandoned New York City building for use as a homeless shelter. All concerned agreed that converting the abandoned building into a homeless shelter was desirable and so the building was sold to the nuns for one dollar. Then came the rules. After one year of bouncing between bureaucrats, the necessary licenses were obtained to begin the renovation. Then came the killer rule: the city required that the nun's building include an elevator. Adding an elevator to a building that had never had one made the project's cost prohibitive. The building remained abandoned and the homeless it might have housed continued to sleep on the streets, all because rules substituted for principles.[7]

King Benjamin recognized the need to be guided by general principles rather than narrow rules. He taught his people that there are so many ways to sin that they cannot be numbered (Mosiah 4:29). Similarly, there are so many ways to do good that God refuses to list them all as individual commandments. Instead, He gives us principles and encourages us to govern ourselves. For example, there is no law that restricts our weight or requires that we brush our teeth at night. Yet, there is a principle that declares that our body is a temple that deserves our careful care. Someone who understands this general principle will come to the conclusion that watching one's weight and brushing one's teeth are good ideas.

If we only followed the formally formulated commandments, we would surely fail to live the gospel completely. We must exert ourselves to do good even without being commanded. Otherwise, we might become like the Levites and priests who passed by the wounded because they were not specifically directed to help (Luke 10:33). The Lord revealed to Joseph Smith:

> For behold, it is not meet that I should command in all things; for he that is compelled in all things, the same is a slothful and not a wise servant; wherefore he receiveth no reward.
>
> Verily I say, men should be anxiously engaged in a good cause, and do many things of their own free will, and bring to pass much righteousness;
>
> For the power is in them, wherein they are agents unto themselves. And inasmuch as men do good they shall in nowise lose their rewards. [D&C 58:26–28]

A friend of mine once declared that "rules are for people without principles." I believe my friend meant that those unwilling to be guided by principles must be restrained by rules. For example, the Israelites under Moses lacked the spiritual maturity to be governed by principles so they were restricted by rules.

Principles and Purposeful Living

Correct principles that connect actions and outcomes provide guides to peaceful living by rescuing order from chaos. The difference between order and chaos is predictability. Suppose every time someone turned on the kitchen faucet something unexpected happened. What if one time turning on the kitchen faucet opened the front door? Or suppose that another time turning on the faucet filled up the bathtub with lemonade? Without an ordered connection between actions and outcomes our lives would not only be chaotic, they would lack purpose. Chaos defeats purposeful living because there can be no realization of a worthy goal unless our choices lead to predictable consequences.

Despite living in a world of ordered connections between actions and outcomes, we can still live private lives of chaos if we are unaware or hold mistaken beliefs about important connections between actions and outcomes. The need to know the connections between actions and outcomes may have motivated Joseph Smith to make his famous statement about principles and self-government. The need to know the consequences of our actions may also explain why the Lord commanded His priesthood to: "teach the principles of my gospel which are in the Bible and the Book of Mormon, in the which is the fullness of the gospel" (D&C 42:12).

Ten principles with promise are described next. These principles promote purposeful living by rescuing order from chaos and produce peace and happiness. These principles include:

1. The principle of restoration: the law of the harvest.

2. The principle of progress: life is a test.

3. The principle of temperance: virtues in perfect balance.

4. The principle of attraction: truth embraceth truth.

5. The principle of conformity: as with the priest, so with the people.

6. The principle of separation: a house divided.

7. The principle of faith: inflated "I" versus divine dependence.

8. The principle of abundance: overcoming pride.

9. The principle of charity: the pure love of Christ.

10. The principle of at-one-ment: after all that we can do.

Elder W. Craig Zwick of the Seventy, one time attended our stake conference and taught that we should teach the gospel the way we learned it. I have tried to follow Elder Zwick's advice in the chapters that follow. In each chapter at least one experience is related that has helped me learn about the principle described. There are, of course, many other principles that could be discussed, but those that follow have special meaning to me and I hope they will be helpful to you.

Chapter One

1 – The Principle of Restoration: The Law of the Harvest

❧

The principle. The principle of restoration declares: *if* you send it out, *then* it will return to you and be restored. The scriptural foundation for this principle is found in Alma's instruction to his onetime wayward son Corianton: "For that which ye do send out shall return unto you again, and be restored" (Alma 41:15).

Somehow my lot in life has been to coach basketball and soccer for the youth leagues organized in my community. My main motive for accepting past coaching assignments has been to spend time with my children who have all been active in sports. My coaching experiences have taught me an important lesson: how well my teams played on Saturday depended on how well they had practiced during the week. This connection between practice and performance is an example of the principle of restoration.

The principle of restoration is the most basic of all gospel principles. Indeed, one may say that all other principles with promise are only special applications of the principle of restoration: what we receive depends on what we give. The principle of restoration confirms that we live in a world of order in which actions produce predictable outcomes so that there are specific consequences to whatever we think about, desire, or do.

Popular expressions that recognize the principle of restoration include: "what goes around comes around;" "you get what you pay for;" "there's no such thing as a free lunch;" "those who play with fire get burned;" and, "don't expect something for nothing." We recognize the principle of restoration in the physical world when we declare that "for every action there is an opposite and equal reaction" and "what goes up must come down."

Ralph Waldo Emerson referred to the principle of restoration when he declared: "The only way to have a friend is to be one."[1] Paul G. Hewitt acknowledged the principle of restoration when he wrote: "If you push hard on the world, the world pushes back on you. If you touch the world gently, the world will touch you gently in return."[2] Abraham Lincoln described the principle of restoration when he declared: "When I do good, I feel good; and when I do bad, I feel bad."[3]

The principle of restoration is taught in the *Old Testament* book of Ecclesiastes. "Cast thy bread upon the waters: for thou shalt find it after many days" (Ecclesiastes 11:1). Limhi taught the principle of restoration when he declared:

> If my people shall sow filthiness they shall reap the chaff thereof in the whirlwind; and the effect thereof is poison.

> And again he saith: If my people shall sow filthiness they shall reap the east wind, which bringeth immediate destruction. [Mosiah 7:30–31]

Alma repeated Limhi's lesson on the principle of restoration when he taught: "For every man receiveth wages of him whom he listeth to obey, and this according to the words of the spirit of prophecy" (Alma 3:27).

The principle of restoration means that when we keep God's commandments we receive God's blessings. This particular application of the principle of restoration was revealed to Joseph Smith, who wrote:

> There is a law, irrevocably decreed in heaven before the foundations of this world, upon which all blessings are predicated.
>
> And when we obtain any blessing from God, it is by obedience to that law upon which it is predicated. [D&C 130:20–21]

King Benjamin added his testimony to those who taught the principle of restoration in his farewell address. "I would desire that ye should consider on the blessed and happy state of those that keep the commandments of God. For behold, they are blessed in all things, both temporal and spiritual; and *if* they hold out faithful to the end [*then*] they are received into heaven, that thereby they may dwell with God in a state of never ending happiness" (Mosiah 2:41; italics added).

One summer Saturday, my wife Bonnie asked me to edge the garden. It was not a difficult task, but I procrastinated until I only had time to complete half of my assignment. The next morning was Sunday and as I arose early and prepared for my assignments, I noticed that my hair length failed to meet reasonable grooming standards. Fortunately, Bonnie had become an expert in trimming my hair. So, in my emergency produced by poor planning, I appealed to her for help. She agreed, but then only trimmed the hair on half of my head. I pleaded for her to finish. I spoke sternly. I promised future favors. But all my efforts to obtain a complete haircut failed. I attended to my church assignments that day with half a haircut. From this I learned one more application of the principle of restoration: as you edge, so are you trimmed.

The Golden Rule and the Principle of Restoration

Because what we send out determines what we receive, the ideal rule governing our behavior is "the golden rule." This rule, included in all major religions of the world, can be stated as: "Therefore, all things whatsoever ye would that men should do to you, do ye even so to them" (3 Nephi 14:12).

Because of the principle of restoration, it follows that the thoughts and feelings we have toward each other are likely to be reciprocated (what goes around comes around). Those we hate will likely hate us and those we love will probably love us in return. If we are kind toward others, they will tend to return our kindness. If we are angry with someone, they will likely become angry with us. If we forgive others their debts, they are likely to forgive us our debts. If we teach others, we will discover additional knowledge and light. If we learn to feel what others are feeling, we will discover that others care about us. If we live virtuously, then we will find increased confidence. As we seek to comfort those in sorrow, we will find relief in our own times of distress. As we allow others their agency even when we have the power to force their compliance, we will discover increased self-control.

Parenting and the Principle of Restoration

Parenting is a process in which order is rescued from chaos by correct principles. Outcomes associated with parental choices, principles, are summarized in an insightful poem by Dorothy Law Nolte, appropriately titled "Children Live What They Learn."

> *If a child lives with criticism, [then] he learns to condemn.*
>
> *If a child lives with hostility, [then] he learns to fight.*
>
> *If a child lives with fears, [then] he learns to be apprehensive.*
>
> *If a child lives with pity, [then] he learns to feel sorry for himself.*
>
> *If a child lives with jealousy, [then] he learns to feel guilty.*
>
> *If a child lives with encouragement, [then] he learns to be confident.*

If a child lives with tolerance, [then] he learns to be patient.

If a child lives with praise, [then] he learns to be appreciative.

If a child lives with acceptance, [then] he learns to love.

If a child lives with approval, [then] he learns to love himself.

If a child lives with recognition, [then] he learns to have a goal.

If a child lives with fairness, [then] he learns what justice is.

If a child lives with honesty, [then] he learns what truth is.

If a child lives with security, [then] he learns to have faith in himself and in those about him.

If a child lives with friendliness, [then] he learns that the world is a good place in which to live.[4]

The Swing Set

Several years ago Ryan, our oldest son, decided to build a large swing set and locate it on our stake farm. The project would complete his requirements to become an Eagle Scout. He purchased large supporting beams and cross pieces and with the help of his friends and family he planned, measured, sawed, drilled holes, attached chains, and transported the entire set of materials to our stake farm. There he assembled the swing set where for several years it served well its purpose. While parents worked on the farm, their children played on the swing set.

Years after the Eagle project had been completed, the stake farm was sold and the swing set was relocated to the Latter-day Saint housing complex adjacent to the campus of Michigan State University. At the complex, a new group of patrons began to enjoy the swing set, the children of the married students living there. In the meantime our oldest son graduated from high school, completed an honorable mission in Southern Utah, married his high school sweetheart, enrolled at Michigan State University, and moved into the Latter-day Saint housing complex. Then their first child was born, a boy named Austin.

When Austin was about two years old, I had an occasion to visit our son and his family at the housing complex. I found our son and daughter-in-law in the playground located in back of their apartment, swinging Austin on our son's Eagle Scout project. What goes around comes around, even if it is in the next generation.

I have since seen the swing set experience repeated in many different settings. In my own life, I enjoyed teaching early morning seminary for several years. One day, I stood before my first college class as a university professor and appreciated the lessons I had learned teaching seminary and thanked the Lord for the preparation. I know of a bishop who in his desire to assist couples resolve marital differences, discovered ways of improving his own marriage. I have watched young men and women leave on their missions and return home with a glow and a goal. I conclude that we will all someday swing on the swing sets we made for others.

The lesson. Because of the principle of restoration, we will experience predictable consequences from all of our choices, but on the Lord's schedule. To receive the blessings God has promised, we must learn and live correct principles.

Chapter Two

2 – The Principle of Progress: Life is a Test

❧

The principle. The principle of progress teaches: *if* we choose the right even when it is difficult, *then* we will progress. Without the opportunity to choose, we remain innocent but we could not progress (2 Nephi 2:23). Fortunately, our Father in Heaven's plan of happiness offers us agency and the opportunity to progress by choosing the right. Sometimes we wear *CTR* rings to remind ourselves to "choose the right." On other occasions we remind ourselves to choose the right by singing, "Choose the right! There is peace in righteous doing; Choose the right! There's safety for the soul" (*Hymns* 239).

Progress, the product of right choices, has a very specific meaning in the gospel plan. It means a steady approach to the likeness of God, accepting new challenges, increasing in knowledge and skill, confessing and eliminating our mistakes, applying newly acquired truths, and increasing the power of each of our facilities. Our progress is intended to follow the Savior's example who "increased in wisdom and stature, and in favour with God and man" (Luke 2:52).

When I was growing up, my mother organized a scrapbook for me that included pictures of my friends and family members and records of significant events. In the front of this book she included a quote from the poet Alfred Lord Tennyson. The quote read: "Happiness is neither this thing nor that, but simply growth." Tennyson understood why progress is important—it is required for our happiness. John A. Widtsoe confirmed the poet's truth when he wrote: "He who finds himself today where he was yesterday is not happy. Stagnation breeds discontent. Men or nations who move onward, whether materially or spiritually, enjoy the greatest joy and daily satisfaction."[1]

Life Is a Test

So that we may progress by making hard choices, our Heavenly Father's plan is organized as a test. He instructed His prophet Abraham: "We will *prove* them herewith, to see if they will do all things whatsoever the Lord their God shall command them" (Abraham 3:25). Another word for *prove* in the Lord's declaration is *test*.

Our test asks each of us: which do you prefer more, the goods of the world or the Kingdom of God? The goods of the world come in the same three packages Satan used to tempt the Savior. These are physical appetites (turn stones into bread), power (command the angels), and riches (all the kingdoms of the world). To all these temptations of the world that appeal to the natural man, the Savior responded: "Get thee hence, Satan: for it is written, Thou shalt worship the Lord thy God, and him only shalt thou serve" (Matthew 4:10).

We, like the Savior, will be tested and asked to make hard choices between the world and the Kingdom. The right answer to all our tests is to seek first the kingdom of God, and His righteousness (Matthew 6:33). Jacob repeated the right answer to our tests when he pleaded: "But before ye seek for riches, seek ye for the kingdom of God" (Jacob 2:18).

We will all face unique tests that ask us to choose between the world and the Kingdom of God. Sometimes our test comes dressed in provocative clothes enticing us to taste the unrighteous. In this case, the right choice is to forsake the forbidden. Sometimes our test comes dressed in dark and despairing garb signaling the loss of a loved one. In this case the right choice is to look through the gloom to that glorious morning when all the graves will be open. Sometimes our test comes dressed in professional attire and calls us away from family and sacred service. In this case the right choice is to put our God and family first. And sometimes our test comes wearing a familiar face of one who should have been a friend and protector but instead abuses and betrays. In this case the right choice is to retain our trust in God and His ability to set all things right again.

Sometimes our test comes dressed in plain clothes and serves simple meals. In this case the right choice is to remember that those who have eternal life are rich. Sometimes our test rides in expensive cars, wears designer clothes, and enjoys the praises of men. In this case the right choice is to remember that God is no respecter of persons and distinguishes between us only by our obedience to His commandments. Sometimes our test appears as a closed door— denying us something we deeply desire. In this case, the right choice is to keep trying to achieve a worthy goal on a new course. Sometimes our test comes dressed like a courier, calling us to tasks for which we feel overwhelmed and under qualified. In this case, the right choice is to take the first step without knowing the end of the journey. And sometimes our test comes dressed like a patient suffering in illness and pain. In this case the right choice is to find something to smile about and others to comfort even when it hurts to do so.

Sometimes our test taking is like being on a journey that asks us to choose alternative roads. Every road we choose means we give up travel on another: "Somewhere ages and ages hence: Two roads diverged in a wood, and I, I took the one less traveled by, And that has made all the difference."[2] On other occasions, our journey does not give us a choice of roads, but only permits us to choose our attitude on a predetermined path.. Another test asks us to accept an assignment to travel through our personalized gardens of grief without becoming bitter.

Elder Neal A. Maxwell described one young girl's test in a general conference address. "[Melissa] Howes' . . . comparatively young father died of cancer several months ago. Just before, Melissa, who was then nine, was voice in family prayer, pleading, 'Heavenly Father, bless my daddy, and if you need him more than us, you can have him. We want him, but Thy will be done. And please help us not to be mad at you'."[3]

What Makes Our Tests Difficult?

Our progress requires that we have the opportunity to make choices. Indeed, as the difficulty of our choices increases, so does our opportunity to progress. Without difficult choices, progress is also difficult. The necessity of difficult choices for our progress is captured by the couplet: "no pain, no gain."

If hard choices are required for our progress, we might ask, what makes our choices difficult? The answer is opposition. Our choices are hard when they are opposed, disputed, fought against, resisted, defied, refused, scorned, confronted, blocked, stymied, cost dearly, or require great sacrifices.

Lehi connected opposition and progress in the following oft quoted verse:

> For it must needs be, that there is an opposition in all things. If not so, my first-born in the wilderness, righteousness could not be brought to pass, neither wickedness, neither holiness nor misery, neither good nor bad. Wherefore, all things must needs be a compound in one; wherefore, if it should be one body it must needs remain as dead, having no life neither death, nor corruption nor incorruption, happiness nor misery, neither sense nor insensibility. [2 Nephi 2:11]

The price we pay to realize our choices measures their difficulty and our opportunity to progress. One person who faced a difficult choice was Joan of Arc. She had to choose between her vision and her life. In Maxwell Anderson's play she declares:

> Every man gives his life for what he believes. Every woman gives
> her life for what she believes. Sometimes people believe in little or
> nothing, and yet they give their lives to that little or nothing. One life
> is all we have, and we live it as we believe in living it, and then it's
> gone. But to surrender what you are and live without belief is more
> terrible than dying—even more terrible than dying young. [4]

Joan of Arc paid for her choice with her life. Joseph Smith paid
for his choice with his life. Most of us face less costly choices. Yet,
many *are* making hard choices. Tens of thousands of young men and
women willingly give up two years of school, socializing, and
entertainment to tell the world the good news that through the
Atonement of Jesus Christ and by making right choices, all mankind
may be saved. Their mission presidents and wives also serve at even
greater costs, often sacrificing their homes, the company of their
families, and even their careers.

What Is the Source of Our Opposition?

Satan uses the gifts of the world that are attractive to our natural
selves to lead us to wrong choices. Yet, these same physical bodies
which are subject to Satan's temptations are essential for us to
experience a fulness of joy. For that reason, it was required that we
come to earth and inherit a physical body. So we are faced with a test,
a contest to determine who will control our physical beings: our
"natural man" desires versus the will of our spirits, one drawn to the
pleasures of the world and the other toward the blessings of the
atonement.

Stephen E. Robinson provided an excellent description of the
opposing forces we all face. Brother Robinson writes that our physical
body "naturally seeks pleasure rather than righteousness because it
has no ability to distinguish between right and wrong— flesh has no
conscience. . . . Just as a thermometer cannot detect radiation and a

Geiger counter cannot detect heat, so our flesh cannot detect light and truth—it wasn't designed to do it. Flesh can distinguish only between pleasure and pain, between 'feels good' and 'doesn't feel good,' and therefore it urges us to act upon that distinction alone."

Continuing, Brother Robinson writes: "Unredeemed and without the guidance of spirit, our flesh is morally blind and is therefore an enemy to God, for Satan can successfully argue to the flesh that sin is pleasurable even when he can't successfully argue to the spirit that sin is right. Consequently, being both incredibly powerful and morally blind, until and unless the carnal self yields to the enticing of the Holy Spirit and accepts the leadership of our own spirit with its moral vision, it remains a loose cannon and an enemy to God (Mosiah 3:19)."[5]

When I was young, my folks kept a pinto mare for me and my brothers and sisters to ride. Her name was Molly and she had a mind of her own. She was a senior citizen among horses and preferred the comfort of her green pasture to long rides outside of town. Thus, Molly required considerable encouragement before she would leave her pasture. Then, if we got Molly bridled and out of her pasture, we faced a new obstacle—keeping her moving. Molly never met a clump of green grass she didn't want to stop and sample. Finally, once we got to the sagebrush and cedar-covered hills beyond town and past the temptations of green grass and her pasture, there was still one more test. It was that if at any moment Molly felt us relax our control, she would immediately turn around and head for home.

I often think of Molly when I consider our physical bodies and our challenge to direct them by yielding to the enticings of the Holy Spirit (Mosiah 3:19). Molly was not evil. There is nothing wrong with sometimes relaxing in the pasture, occasionally stopping to munch grass, or even at some point ending a trip—except when it is contrary to the will of the rider on one's back. Similarly, the desires of our physical bodies are not evil unless exercised outside of the bounds the Lord has set.

Horses and our physical bodies can both be the source of much joy if we can control them. Our progress demands that we both bridle horses and our passions. Alma taught: "Bridle all your passions, that ye may be filled with love" (Alma 38:12).

Finally, there is one more lesson that I learned from Molly. When my Dad rode Molly, she never challenged him like she did me. He was clearly in control and where Dad directed, Molly went. Molly submitted to Dad's will because she had learned that Dad was in control.

The relationship between our physical bodies and our spirits can be like that which exists between a horse and a small boy or a strong man. When the rider's will wins, the horse soon learns to submit. But when the horse's will wins, the horse becomes more demanding. Similarly, when we give in to the desires of our physical appetites beyond the bounds the Lord has set, they become more demanding. When our spirits dominate the desires of the natural man, the natural man learns to submit and future victories over the body become easier. Shakespeare summarized the power over the flesh that comes from resisting temptation when he had his character Hamlet declare:

> *Refrain to-night;*
> *And that shall lend a kind of easiness*
> *To the next abstinence, the next more easy;*
> *For use almost can change the stamp of nature,*
> *And either master the devil or throw him out*
> *With wondrous potency.*[6]

Difficult Choices and Progress

How does opposition to our righteous choices provide opportunities for growth? The answer is really quite simple. When we are faced with opposition, we are forced to try harder. Then, as we make increased effort, several progressive events may occur.

Consider the experience of Joseph Smith. Joseph retired to a grove of trees to ask God which of all the sects is right? He records that as he offered up his prayer he was opposed by a power that overcame him, bound his tongue, and covered the area around him in thick darkness. In response to the opposing power of his enemy, Joseph records that he exerted all his powers to call upon God (JS–H, 1:15, 16). Could it be that it was Joseph's increased effort required by the powerful opposition of his enemy that made possible the visit of the Father and Son in the Sacred Grove? Consider other blessings that we may earn by meeting well those forces that oppose our righteous choices.

We develop capacities and power that we didn't have before. I remember my first talk in Sunday School. My uncle Gene was there and I wanted to make a good impression. But when I stood up to speak, I froze. I couldn't remember a word of my talk and after a minute of painful silence, I ran home crying. Years later and after hundreds of talks, I believe I give better talks; at least I don't run home crying now.

We discover capacities and power that we didn't know before. I have watched and coached several sporting contests. In those events, I have learned one remarkable lesson: teams tend to rise to the level of their opposition. Bill Russell, a former player for the Boston Celtics, described the need for opposition to play his best. "Every so often a Celtic game would heat up so that it became more than a physical or even mental game, and would be magical . . . When it happened I could feel my play rise to a new level. It came rarely, and would last anywhere from five minutes to a whole quarter or more . . . It would surround not only me and the other Celtics but also the players on the other team, and even the referees. To me, the key was that *both* teams had to be playing at their peaks, and they had to be competitive."[7]

I recently watched a public television program that included interviews with former prisoners of the Viet Nam War. I was impressed with one interview of a prisoner who had suffered through years of cruel torture. When asked how he survived he responded: "We never know our strengths until pushed to our limits."

We face weaknesses that before were hidden. My oldest son recently completed his training to become a nurse. Before he could practice, he was required to take a state licensing exam. At the time he sat for the exam, he said he believed he was adequately prepared. The exam results confirmed he was not fully prepared. He failed the exam. As a result of the failed exam, he was forced to make some painful searches for weaknesses. He asked: what more could I have done? In what areas am I unprepared? Do I really want to be a nurse? Then he resolved to better prepare for the next opportunity to take the state exam. He took practice exams. He focused on areas in which he had scored low. He visited with others who had successfully taken the exam and asked them how they had prepared. He then spent many additional hours studying. The result was he passed his next try with high marks. His opposition in the form of a failed exam caused him to first identify a weakness and then to replace it with a strength.

We acknowledge we need help and in our humility discover our Savior. In the face of extreme opposition we may often come to know that we cannot make it on our own and then in our humility, we discover the goodness and the greatness of God. Joseph Smith faced extreme opposition that led to his imprisonment in Liberty Jail where he cried out: "O God, where art thou?" (D&C 121:1). In that moment when the forces of the adversary were combined against him, Joseph Smith came to know again the Savior who responded to his plea: "My son, peace be unto thy soul: thine adversity and thine afflictions shall be but a small moment; and then, if thou endure it well, God shall exalt thee on high; thou shalt triumph over all thy foes" (D&C 121:7–8). We too may come to know God in the face of opposition and find our love for Him increase and our desire to serve him magnified.

Finally, when faced with opposition that tests our souls and tries our patience, we gain empathy for others who are suffering in similar ways. As we gain empathy for others we progress in our ability to aid others and in the process gain an important Christlike virtue. Alma, writing about the Savior declared: "he will take upon him their infirmities, that his bowels may be filled with mercy, according to the flesh, that he may know according to the flesh how to succor his people according to their infirmities" (Alma 7:12).

I have found that most virtues are discovered and acquired during our most difficult moments. Thus, the opposition that we would avoid if possible is often our best friend. This theme was echoed in a poem quoted by Spencer W. Kimball, who was personally acquainted with much opposition.

> Pain stayed so long I said to him today,
> "I will not have you with me any more."
> I stamped my foot and said, "Be on your way,"
> And paused there, startled at the look he wore.
> "I, who have been your friend," he said to me,
> "I, who have been your teacher—all you know
> Of understanding, love, of sympathy
> And patience, I have taught you. Shall I go?"
> He spoke the truth, this strange unwelcome guest;
> I watched him leave, and knew that he was wise.
> He left a heart grown tender in my breast,
> He left a far, clear vision in my eyes.
> I dried my tears, and lifted up a song—
> Even for one who'd tortured me so long.[8]

What Is the Source of Our Opposition?

Without opposition, there are no hard choices to make and "righteousness could not be brought to pass, neither wickedness, neither holiness nor misery, neither good nor bad" (2 Nephi 2:11). But opposition can come from several sources. First, it sometimes comes from the choices others make. Second, it sometimes comes from the natural churnings of mortality. Third, it sometimes comes from divine intervention. And fourth, it sometimes comes from our own choices.

Opposition created by the choices of others. I am in the process of writing this book a second time—from the beginning. A few years ago I was in the Miami Florida airport. A traveling companion was watching my bags, one of which contained my personal computer with a completed version of this book stored separately on the computer's hard drive and on external disks. Unfortunately, someone else was also watching our bags. In a brief moment during which my companion turned away, someone stole my bag and my completed book.

I couldn't believe it. The stolen book represented years of work and for some months I couldn't bring myself to begin writing this book a second time. Yet, I felt divine comfort that the project could be completed again. A visit with my friend, a computer programmer, also helped. He concluded that it was probably a good thing that my book was lost. He explained that sometimes when he and his colleagues need to revise a computer program, they sometimes throw the old one away and write a new one. It seems that sometimes a revised program can never be made as efficient as a new one that begins with the solution in mind and benefits from lessons learned and mistakes made in the first attempt.

So I began to write this book again. In the process of trying harder to write this book, I made several discoveries that helped me progress. First, I discovered that the mind has an amazing ability to recall information we once knew. Second, I discovered that writing improves with rewriting. Third, and finally, I became acquainted with the person willing to start writing a book a second time from the beginning.

Opposition created by the churning of mortality. A second source of opposition results from the natural churnings of mortality. Mortality is laced with natural forms of opposition. Our bodies have natural limitations and desires that often oppose our choices. Any skill we acquire demands practice. Meeting our material needs requires work. A healthy body in the future often requires exercise today and sore muscles tomorrow.

Mortality with all its physical experiences and connections often defines the cost of our choices. Giving birth, my wife assures me, is a painful process. But the mother's pain is required to begin life. Death can also be a painful process, especially for those suffering painful illnesses and for the lonely loved ones left behind. Aging also alters the cost of our choices as we experience increasing physical limitations.

One day I was in my front yard visiting with my elderly neighbor who was recovering from a severe heart attack. I asked her how she was getting along. She quoted a popular comedian who once declared: "Getting old isn't for sissies." I believe the comedian's quote could be applied more generally. We cannot be sissies and live life well. We must choose the right even when it is difficult to do so.

Opposition and divine intervention. A third source of opposition is divine interventions. God does on occasion intervene in ways that alter the costs of our choices. In the days of Noah God sent the rains; in the days of Elijah the Tishbite God sent a drought; and in the days of the early pioneers, God sent the seagulls. Surely we would not rule out divine interventions that alter the cost of our choices, else why pray for them?

Still, there are important occasions when God does not intervene to reduce the cost of our choices. Amulek implored Alma to stretch forth his hands and with God's power prevent the martyrdom of the newly converted. Alma responded:

> The Spirit constraineth me that I must not stretch forth mine hand; for behold the Lord receiveth them up unto himself, in glory; and he doth suffer that they may do this thing, or that the people may do this thing unto them, according to the hardness of their hearts, that the judgments which he shall exercise upon them in His wrath may be just; and the blood of the innocent shall stand as a witness against them, yea, and cry mightily against them at the last day. [Alma 14:11]

While I cannot fathom God's criteria for intervening in our trials, fatherhood has taught me the importance of limiting my interventions in the lives of my children so they can sometimes make hard choices. I remember one day many years ago watching my oldest son playing in a sand box shared by the families living in our student housing complex. An older boy arrived at the sand box and started pouring sand on our son's head. I was incensed and was ready to run to our son's relief. But I was impressed to wait and see how he would deal with this sand box delinquent. He handled it just fine. He moved to a different spot in the sand box and the problem was solved.

Because I did not intervene, our son learned to deal with bigger boys. (Later he acquired some wrestling skills that worked well, too.) Maybe the bigger boy learned that you don't make friends by pouring sand on people, a lesson he might not have learned if he were restricted. I learned that it is sometimes necessary to suffer on the sideline so that growth can occur on the playing field. So while it may sometimes appear that the Lord has abandoned us in our moments of trial, He has not. He patiently waits for us to grow through our hard choices well made.

Opposition and our own choices. Finally, our own choices often create opposition that increases the cost of future choices. One person wisely noted that most of what we learn comes from experiences that were created by our poor choices.

I once had two good friends who once were husband and wife but who mistreated each other. Then despite the best efforts of friends and family members, they divorced. While the divorce ended the marriage of this former companionship, it also created new costs and additional hard choices. First, the wife and children moved from their previous home into a small apartment where they were forced to face life with reduced financial resources. Then the parents faced reduced opportunities to grow with their children and often spent time alone. But I believe their most difficult tasks were trying to relieve the emotional burden of their children, who somehow felt responsible for the chaos in which they were now living.

Tests and Consequences

When opposition follows from our wrong choices, we may need to repent and choose a different road. But when opposition comes not as a consequence of our choices, but as a result of others' choices, life's churnings, or God's intervention, our response should not be self-condemnation or even a course correction. Instead we should appeal to God for strength and wisdom to continue the journey on the right road.

Our peace in this life requires that we recognize the difference between consequences that follow from our choices, and tests created by opposing forces that are required for our discovery and development. We may experience unnecessary anxiety if every time a painful experience occurs we assume it is a consequence of our own poor choices. To help us distinguish between tests and consequences, the Lord was careful to point out examples of contrasting experiences—one a consequence of a choice and the other a test.

Jesus once passed by a blind man, and His disciples asked: "Master, who did sin, this man or his parents, that he was born blind?"

Jesus answered, that neither the man nor his parents had sinned (John 9:1–2). The man's blindness, the Savior taught, was not a consequence of an evil deed, but opposition allowing the man to demonstrate discipleship in the face of adversity. On another occasion, the Savior healed an invalid and later instructed him: "sin no more, lest a worse thing come unto thee" (John 5:14). In this instance the man's affliction may have been connected to sin and consistent with the principle of restoration.

Job suffered unusually strong winds of opposition that his friends assumed were restored to him for some evil deed. But Job recognized that he was being tested, not punished, and responded to his spiritually blind friends: "But [God] knoweth the way that I take: when he hath tried me, I shall come forth as gold" (Job 23:10). We, like Job, will all experience outcomes unconnected to our actions. These will try our faith. Nephi attempted to prepare us for these when he wrote:

> But behold, the righteous, the saints of the Holy One of Israel, they who have believed in the Holy One of Israel, they who have endured the crosses of the world, and despised the shame of it, they shall inherit the kingdom of God, which was prepared for them from the foundation of the world, and their joy shall be full forever. [2 Nephi 9:18]

The apostle Peter instructed the early Christians to distinguish between tests and consequences. This, Peter taught, requires that we sometimes bear patiently the outcomes not of our making. He taught: "For what glory is it, if when ye be buffeted for your faults, ye shall take it patiently? But if, when ye do well, and suffer for it, ye take it patiently, this is acceptable with God" (1 Peter 2:20). About the tests we must face in this world, the Psalmist wrote: "many are the afflictions of the righteous: but the Lord delivereth him out of them all" (Psalm 34:19). And Christ declared: "These things I have spoken unto you, that in me ye might have peace. In the world ye shall have tribulation: but be of good cheer; I have overcome the world" (John 16:33).

Elder Richard G. Scott confirmed the considerable difference between tests and consequences. He taught that some adversity we face is caused by our transgression of the laws of God that requires humble repentance. Elder Scott then added: "The other reason for adversity is to accomplish the Lord's own purposes in our life that we may receive the refinement that comes from testing. It is vital for each of us to identify from which of these two sources come our trials and challenges, because correct responses to tests and consequences can be very different."[9]

Is the Test Fair?

Clear connections between actions and outcomes confirm our confidence in the principle of restoration. An employee works hard and is promoted and appreciated by her employer. A mother and father teach and follow correct principles and their children grow up faithful members of the church. Workers live frugally and save during their working years and when they retire have enough money to serve missions, travel, and spoil their grandchildren. But what about those outcomes we experience that appear to be unrelated to our actions? These may challenge our confidence in the principle of restoration and lead us to question God's justice.

Some outcomes unconnected to our actions are unearned blessings. We communicate over long distances, listen to recorded sound, view recorded vistas, and light up the dark with inventions others created. We travel in cars we did not assemble, eat food we did not grow, and fly in airplanes we did not design. We are protected from diseases by vaccines that were produced in experiments we did not conduct. We enjoy freedoms won in battles we did not fight. Finally, we enjoy material prosperity that would surpass the dreams of ancient kings because of production practices we did not organize. For these unearned blessings and countless others, we owe thanks to the likes of Alexander Graham Bell, Thomas Edison, Henry Ford, Gregor

Mendel, Orville and Wilbur Wright, Jonathan Salk, Dwight Eisenhower, and Eli Whitney.

Other outcomes unconnected to our actions are undeserved hardships. A drive-by shooter kills an innocent child in Los Angeles. A mentally disturbed mother in North Carolina drowns her two helpless children. Terrorists maim and murder men, women, and children in New York City. A Michigan investor betrays his clients and leaves them unprepared for retirement. An adulterous husband leaves his devoted wife for a younger woman. A depraved parent abuses his defenseless children. Religious fanatics burn alive three small children in Northern Ireland. Finally, devoted parents live exemplary lives and faithfully teach the gospel to their children only to see them forsake their faith.

Several years ago I visited a friend whose wife had just died of cancer after a prolonged illness. After our visit and in response to my effort to provide comfort, he summarized his life's view with the words: "life is not fair." I think he was saying, if life were fair, how could this tragedy occur to someone as good and kind as my wife? It appeared to him that his wife's suffering and death at a young age were unconnected to the way she had lived and inconsistent with the principle of restoration.

Perhaps my friend's problem was he failed to distinguish between tests and consequences of our choices. The principle of restoration promises that predictable consequences will follow our actions. It does not promise that our only experiences will be those connected to our own choices. The rain, it seems, falls uninvited on the parades of both the just and unjust.

But even if we make the distinction between tests and consequences, how can we explain the considerable differences in our tests? Some live healthy and long lives while others live short and painful ones. Is God responsible for the suffering that so often accompanies our tests? Could He alter our tests by reducing the opposition if He chose to and limit the bad things that happen to good people? And if He could stop bad things happening to good people, why doesn't He?

I do not know what determines our tests. I do have confidence, however, that if we knew what determines our test, we would not believe them to be unfair. I also believe that our tests are related to our needs for discovery and development. When the plan of progress was proposed along with its required tests, we shouted for joy. While we now can't remember what all the shouting was about, we one time accepted it with joy and enthusiasm (Job 38:7).

Perhaps it would be easier for us to accept our hard choices if there were not so many who believe that our tests should be easy and that virtue can be acquired without a price.[10] We are introduced to this distortion of reality early on in fairy tales when at the end of the story we are told that the hero and heroine lived happily ever after. Eliza R. Snow attempted to teach the saints that even in Zion, life is a test and that our progress is earned with a price. She penned the hymn whose first verse teaches:

> *Think not when you gather to Zion,*
> *Your troubles and trials are through,*
> *That nothing but comfort and pleasure*
> *Are waiting in Zion for you? :*
> *No, no, 'tis designed as a furnace,*
> *All substance, all textures to try,*
> *To burn all the "wood, hay, and stubble,"*
> *The gold from the dross purify.*[11]

The Principles of Restoration and Growth

Of course, it is necessary to distinguish between consequences and tests to differentiate between the principle of restoration and the principle of growth. It is also important to recognize that for tests to occur, it is sometimes necessary for the full consequences of our choices to be delayed. One can imagine that life's tests would not be tests at all if the consequences of our choices occurred at the moment of decision. Thus, some blessings and some curses associated with our choices may be delayed, even until the next life.

The Savior exemplified this delayed connection between choices and consequences. During his tests in Gethsemane and Golgotha, He suffered beyond what any mortal can imagine. Yet, the joyful consequences of that choice were not realized until after His resurrection. Only after His resurrection and appearance before the Nephites where He witnessed their humility and faith did He declare: "now my joy is full" (3 Nephi 17:20).

Passing Our Tests

Life's tests have the power to refine or dull our spiritual senses depending on our choices. Consider the differences between those who suffered through the same wars. "because of the exceedingly great length of the war between the Nephites and the Lamanites *many* had become hardened, because of the exceedingly great length of the war; and *many* were softened because of their afflictions, insomuch that they did humble themselves before God, even in the depth of humility" (Alma 62:41; italics added).

Passing our tests means that we emerge from the classroom still preferring the kingdom of God and trusting in His goodness. One who emerged from a difficult test with passing grades was Job, who despite suffering great costs declared: "Though he [God] slay me, yet will I trust him" (Job 13:15). Failing the test means we emerge hard hearted —angry at God and disappointed in mankind (and often at ourselves).

The good news is that we can pass our tests without becoming bitter and disappointed—but we need God's help. Alma taught: "humble yourselves before the Lord, and call on His holy name, and watch and pray continually, that ye may not be tempted above that which ye can bear, and thus be led by the Holy Spirit, becoming humble, meek, submissive, patient, full of love and all long-suffering" (Alma 13:28).

My family and I know an unusual man who faced hard tests and emerged victorious. In a recent cover story in our local newspaper the man is pictured wrestling with our youngest son. The story describes how he volunteers his time to teach area high school wrestlers. Recently, two of the wrestlers he tutored won state championships. One of the wrestlers was quoted as saying that he owed his career to this good man. Every summer this man and his wife donate hundreds of dollars in scholarships plus their own time so that wrestlers can attend summer camps. One parent of a wrestler was quoted as saying that this coach is a role model for the young men he coaches and that his real goal is to prepare them for responsible citizenship.[12]

What is remarkable about this story is that about 11 years ago this volunteer wrestling coach was living in Northern Michigan, married, and enjoying an elementary school teaching career. Then he noticed his already poor eyesight was failing. After a checkup, his doctor informed him he would soon lose his eyesight completely. Then he and his wife divorced and the school where he was working terminated his employment.

He responded by moving from Michigan to Baltimore, Maryland where he enrolled at the Johns Hopkins University, which offered computer training for the blind. While in Baltimore he met and married his charming companion. His training eventually led him to what has been a very successful career in data systems analysis and allowed him to return to the State of Michigan and to locate in our area—and you know the rest of the story. He faced difficult tests that were not the result of his actions with courage and good cheer. The outcomes that have followed his good deeds have been predictable.

The Lesson

The rains of opposition fall on the just and unjust and determine the costs of our choices. We must make hard choices created by opposition if we are to discover and develop our better selves. Viewing opposition as an ingredient required for our progress should change our response to life's tests. Instead of viewing opposition as a stern school master whose difficult tests may prevent us from a glorious graduation, we should see opposition as a friend who encourages us to climb higher for a better view.

Chapter Three

3 – The Principle of Temperance: Virtues in Perfect Balance

✎∽

The principle. Temperance means balance. The opposite of temperance is excess or an absence of balance. Virtue is a general moral excellence. A practical definition of virtue is a quality possessed by the Savior. The principle of temperance explains: *if* we are to become like Christ, *then* we must seek for virtues in balanced or equally developed pairs. The Savior is full of justice and mercy, kindness and firmness, comfort and direction, patience and sense of urgency, humility and confidence, and joy and sorrow. President Ezra Taft Benson declared: "Nearly two thousand years ago a perfect Man walked the earth—Jesus the Christ. He was the Son of a Heavenly Father and an earthly mother. He is the God of this world, under the Father. In his life, all the virtues were lived and kept in perfect balance."[1]

Alma taught his son Shiblon that: "I would that ye would be diligent and temperate in all things" (Alma 38:10). And in revelations given through Joseph Smith, the Lord instructed that those who assist in His work must be temperate in all things (D&C 12:8) and that all things given to man were to be used: "with judgment, not to excess, neither by extortion" (D&C 59:20).

A few minutes from where I grew up in Fillmore, Utah runs Chalk Creek, or what we always referred to as "the crick." There were no serviceable bridges over the creek near my home, which wasn't a problem most of the year when the creek was dry. But during the spring and early summer, melting snow and rain raised the creek's water level and made it a considerable challenge to cross. So during the high water period, my friends and I mostly attempted our crossings using rocks that rose above the rushing waters. It was quite a trick to hop from one rock to another without falling in. We all learned that a dry crossing required that we maintain our balance. Leaning too far to one side while perched on a rock meant a walk in the water and soggy socks and shoes.

We need temperance or spiritual balance to meet life's tests just like my friends and I needed physical balance to cross Chalk Creek during high water. Temperance requires maintaining a position between extremes, not too fast and not too slow, not too high and not too low, not too hot and not too cold, not too meek and not too bold. A mental picture of temperance is that of the circus performer who walks across a high wire suspended in the air. The secret to the performer's successful journey is the long pole that she carries with its weight equally balanced on each side of the wire. Another mental picture of temperance is that of the chef who adds just the right amount of seasoning to his main dish. Too little or too much seasoning would spoil his meal since the seasoning must be balanced by the other ingredients.

One night, our daughter Rachel and I were driving home from out of town and stopped at a restaurant for a sandwich. I like a good Reuben sandwich. The place we stopped had one on their menu advertised as a mile high Reuben. I ordered it. It was not a mile high and not all that good either. Their advertisement was extreme and exaggerated the truth. Extremes distort the truth and convert refreshments into gluttony.

Spiritual Synergism

Like ingredients in a perfectly balanced recipe, like players on a team who each performs her part in harmony with other team members, like an orchestra whose players balance their music with each other, we too must develop and practice our virtues in perfect balance. The Lord desires that we seek for virtues in perfect balance because then our efforts will be multiplied or synergistic. Balanced virtues are synergistic because they magnify each other's desirable properties and produce results greater than the sum of their individual efforts. The Lord recognizes our need for balance and commands we seek for virtues in complementary combinations. For example, the Ten Commandments achieve a balance between commandments to worship God and commandments to respect man. Consider some other examples of commandments to obtain virtues in balanced pairs.

On one occasion the Lord commanded his servants to reprove on occasion with sharpness but immediately thereafter to balance the reproof with an increase in love (D&C 121: 43). Specific corrections followed with an increase in love are synergistic because they both guide and encourage. Correction and love are synergistic. One without the other is inadequate. Another command for balance is implied in the Lord's instruction that "neither is the man without the woman nor the woman without the man in the Lord." The different qualities of men and women are required for balance and when combined are synergistic.

A perfect example of balance and synergy is the human body. The body is not one member, but many, and its proper functioning depends on a balanced effort of all of its parts. For example, the eye cannot say to the hand, I have no need of you; nor, can the head say to the feet, I have no need of you. All are needed because God has tempered the body together (1 Corinthians 12:14, 21, 24). A Zion people also illustrate the synergy obtained through proper balance between their hearts, minds, and hands. Zion could not be built without the balance between their understanding obtained in their minds, their love of each other that resides in their hearts, and their work and service performed by their hands. As a result, they live righteously and have no poor among them (Moses 7:18).

Synergy produced by balanced virtues is easy to recognize by considering what happens to balanced pairs of virtues when separated. For example, faith is important and so are good works. But faith without works is dead and work without faith lacks direction. Faith balanced with good works has both the vision and the energy needed to bless lives and build Zion. Honesty is important and so is kindness. But kindness without honesty may fail to provide needed corrections while honesty without kindness lacks the caring that motivates a course correction. Kindness balanced with honesty gives both direction and caring that encourages a redirected effort.

In his book, *In Perfect Balance*, Elder Spencer J. Condie of the Seventy discusses the need for balance. He cites the need for balance between mercy and justice, faith and works, risk and security, form and content, the spirit of the law and the letter of the law, steadfastness and change, initiative and obedience, reproof and reconciliation, good cheer and solemnity, boldness and meekness, loyalty to principles and loyalty to persons, communication and confidentiality, remembering and forgetting, the physical and the spiritual, and learning and teaching.[2]

The need for temperance can be understood by comparing it to a journey. Any successful journey requires that we travel in the right direction. This is the test of opposites, the focus of the previous chapter. But besides the test of opposites is the test of temperance that requires that we not only travel in the right direction but that we also travel the right distance, not too near and not too far.

A poignant example of a failed temperance test of traveling the right distance involved the Willie and Martin handcart companies. These companies left Florence (Omaha), Nebraska late in the summer of 1856 for a journey West. Early snows slowed their progress and eventually they halted in the rugged Wyoming wilderness. When Brigham Young learned of their plight, he sent relief wagons to their aid. The first relief party under George D. Grant first found the Willie company and later the Martin company. But subsequent relief efforts traveled in the right direction to accomplish their mission but halted and began returning before they reached the stranded travelers. Especially the Martin company continued to suffer because later parties failed to travel the needed distance even though they had traveled in the right direction. A successful journey requires both the correct direction and the right distance.

Temperance Versus Excess

Besides producing synergy, another reason to seek for temperance is to prevent our virtues from being pulled or pushed to extremes. It was once said of Winston Churchill that his vices were extreme forms of his virtues. That expression generally applies to all of us. Our virtues pushed or pulled to excess become vices. Temperance prunes our virtues and keeps them from growing into vices.

To understand how a virtue pushed to an excess may become a vice, consider the economic principle of diminishing returns. The principle of diminishing returns explains that inputs applied beyond some optimal level will produce diminishing returns. To illustrate, imagine the satisfaction provided by an ice cream treat consumed on a warm summer's day. Then consider the satisfaction provided by additional ice cream treats consumed immediately after the first one. One might still enjoy the second ice cream treat, but not likely the third, and definitely not the fourth or fifth. Each additional treat produces less satisfaction than the first and at some point additional treats are not desired at all. Similarly, a virtue pushed to an extreme may produce a sensation much like eating too much ice cream.

President Boyd K. Packer taught the need for balance and the danger of excess by comparing the gospel to a piano keyboard. "Some members of the Church who should know better pick out a hobby key or two and tap them incessantly, to the irritation of those around them. They can dull their own spiritual sensitivities. They lose track that there is a fulness of the gospel . . . [which they reject] in preference to a favorite note. This becomes exaggerated and distorted, leading them away into apostasy."[3]

In a powerful warning message against gospel piano key tapping, Dallin H. Oaks warned that our strengths can become our weaknesses when pushed to an extreme. Elder Oaks pointed out that Satan not only attacks our weaknesses but also our strengths. For example, a member may have an unusual commitment to one particular doctrine or commandment of the gospel of Jesus Christ such as family history work, or constitutional government. But these specialized interests may become a weakness if they prevent us from seeking other truths. The very real danger of gospel specialization is that we become like the members of the Shaker sect who "desire to know the truth in part, but not all" (D&C 49:2).[4]

Examples of virtues pushed to their undesirable extremes follow. Justice is a virtue. But justice that travels too far and pushed to an extreme becomes punishment unless balanced by mercy. Mercy is a virtue. But mercy that travels too far and pushed to an extreme becomes indulgence.

Honesty is a virtue. But honesty that travels too far and pushed to an extreme becomes insensitive and uncaring unless balanced by kindness. Kindness is a virtue. But kindness that travels too far and pushed to an extreme becomes flattery.

Financial responsibility is a virtue. But financial responsibility that travels too far and pushed to an extreme becomes stingy unless balanced by generosity. But generosity that travels too far and pushed to an extreme becomes an unwise steward.

Humility that recognizes one's dependence on God is a virtue. Yet humility that travels too far and pushed to an extreme fails to undertake any independent action unless balanced by self-confidence. But self-confidence that travels too far and pushed to an extreme becomes pride that believes one succeeded all by himself.

Finally, some might argue that excellence requires an extreme effort. A related argument is that all greatness is characterized by a focused or an unbalanced life. Supporting this critique is the quip that in attempting to become a jack of all trades, we becoming a master of none. This line of reasoning, however, ignores the many ways that balance can be achieved. For example, sometimes balance can be achieved by combining our skills with others to obtain a common goal. In this regard we become members of a team. As a member of the team, balance is achieved by players combining their specialized talents. The team needs several players to achieve balance and no one player is expected to perform in all positions.

The Celestial Rule

In preparing to write this chapter and having read the references referred to earlier, I wondered if there was a principal balance that is required in our efforts to obtain virtues in balancing pairs? The gospel teaches that there is one. We are directed to balance our requests from God with our service to his children. We call this balance the celestial balance.

The scriptural basis directing us to strive for celestial balance is: "Therefore, all things whatsoever ye would that God should do to you, do ye even so to men" (adapted from 3 Nephi 14:12). The Savior emphasized the need for celestial balance when He instructed the Nephites to forgive one another so they could receive forgiveness from their Father in Heaven (3 Nephi 13:11; Matthew 6:12). Christ taught His disciples the importance of celestial balance rule when He explained how one qualifies to sit on His favored right side. Christ explained:

> For I was an hungered, and ye gave me meat: I was thirsty, and ye gave me drink: I was a stranger, and ye took me in:
>
> Naked, and ye clothed me: I was sick and ye visited me: I was in prison, and ye came unto me. [Matthew 25:35–36]

And when did they do such deeds, asked His disciples? The Lord responded: "Inasmuch as ye have done it unto one of the least of these my brethren, ye have done it unto me" (Matthew 25:40).

Thus it does appear that the blessings we receive from God depend on our service to God's children, our own brothers and sisters.

The requirements of celestial balance are described in the first and second great commandments, to love God with all of our hearts, might, mind, and strength and to love our neighbors as ourselves. Other expressions of the celestial balance include King Benjamin's counsel that when ye are in the service of your fellow man, you are only in the service of your God (Mosiah 2:17). Celestial balance is reflected in Jacob's counsel to seek first the kingdom of God, and then seek the riches of the world to bless others (Jacob 2:17–19). The Lord taught His missionaries the importance of celestial balance when He commanded them to seek first to obtain His word and only then to declare it and share it with others (D&C 11:21).

The Savior emphasized celestial balance when he taught:

> But I say unto you, that whosoever is angry with his brother shall be in danger of his judgment. And whosoever shall say to his brother, Raca, shall be in danger of the council; and whosoever shall say, thou fool, shall be in danger of hell fire.
>
> Therefore, if ye shall come unto me, or shall desire to come unto me, and rememberest that thy brother hath aught against thee—
>
> Go thy way unto thy brother, and first be reconciled to thy brother,

and then come unto me with full purpose of heart, and I will receive you. [3 Nephi 12:22–24]

Finally, to emphasize the important balance required between His grace and our service to others, He commanded:

> A new commandment I give unto you, That ye love one another; as I have loved you, that ye also love one another.
>
> By this shall men know that ye are my disciples, if ye have love one to another. [John 13:34–35]

Recognizing the essential balance needed in our relationship between God and man helps us answer one important question: how can I recognize balancing virtues? The answer is, balancing virtues generally involves having one virtue connected to the divine and the other to our work in mortality.

Physical work is a virtue, but unless balanced by meditation that sanctifies one's efforts, it can become drudgery. Study and prayer may bring us spiritual enlightenment but that enlightenment will be of little benefit to others unless balanced by good works of service in which what is learned is shared in family home evening, a home teaching visit, or a Sunday school lesson. Being patient with our fellow travelers, who on occasion jostle us on our journey through life, can teach us patience if we are steadied by the peace the gospel brings. Assisting financially in building the kingdom through the payment of tithes and fast offering is a righteous act but an act that sanctifies only if our payments are accompanied by thanksgiving for God's grace that sent the rains and the worldly success from which our harvest was gathered.

Elder L. Tom Perry recently provided an example of Celestial balance. He reported attending a priesthood class in a rural Wyoming community where a well-prepared instructor taught receptive students the principles of justification and sanctification. After the instruction was complete, one member of the class remarked that the instruction was wonderful but likely to be forgotten unless applied. Then this quorum member reported on the death of a member of their community. This man's death left his widow without means of harvesting the crops. The quorum agreed to assist the widow harvest her crops. After organizing their assistance, Elder Perry remarked that one member of the quorum observed: "This project is just what we needed as a group to work together again."[5] By serving the widow, the priesthood brothers achieved a balance between hearing the word of God and serving a grieving widow.

The Lesson

The Lord's people live virtuous lives by acquiring the Savior's qualities in balancing pairs. Failure to develop virtues in balancing pairs may sometimes permit our virtues to grow into excesses and vices. Regarding our need for balance, President Gordon B. Hinckley counseled: "The major work of the world is not done by geniuses. It is done by ordinary people, with balance in their lives, who have learned to work in an extraordinary manner."[6]

We are not expected to be perfect all at once. Even our effort to acquire virtues in balancing pairs requires balance. To acquire virtues in balancing pairs is like climbing a mountain. It was never intended that we would attempt the climb alone nor to climb faster than we have strength. It was always intended that when we were tired we would lean on Him. The formula is to lean on the Lord and to extend one's hand to lift another. Grace and good works will see us to the top.

Chapter Four

4 – The Principle of Attraction: Truth Embraceth Truth

❧

The principle. The principle of attraction predicts: *if* individuals are similar, *then* they will be attracted to each other and drawn toward similar places, and things. The reason for the attraction of similar people to each other is simple. We find comfort with those who are most like us and who do not require that we defend our differences. The scriptural foundation for the principle of attraction is found in a revelation given to the prophet Joseph Smith in which the Lord declared: "For intelligence cleaveth unto intelligence; wisdom receiveth wisdom; truth embraceth truth; virtue loveth virtue; light cleaveth unto light; mercy has compassion on mercy and claimeth her own; justice continueth its course and claimeth its own; judgment goeth before the face of him who sitteth upon the throne and governeth and executeth all things" (D&C 88:40).

Scientists have long recognized that similar plants and trees are attracted to the same climates. Grains grow well in Kansas and cotton prospers in Texas. New England produces beautiful hardwoods, and apples shine in the state of Washington. This natural tendency for similar plants and trees to be attracted to the same climate has a parallel. People with similar spiritual tendencies are attracted to the same spiritual climates and to each other. The tendency for similar people to attract each other and to be attracted to similar environments is called here the principle of attraction.

The Principle of Attraction and Self-judgment

The principle of attraction teaches an important lesson. We judge ourselves by our attractions. When we enjoy the companionship of the Holy Ghost and seek for the sacred and divine, we are pure. When we are drawn to the worldly and the pleasures of the natural man, we are at that moment of the world. So, we judge ourselves by our choice of friends to whom we are attracted. Some years ago a public-opinion research firm asked 2007 people to identify one or two things that said the most about themselves. Friends far outranked homes, jobs, clothes and cars.[1]

I have watched with interest the principle of attraction applied to the changing circle of our children's friends. In their early years they had much in common with their playmates from other faiths and were often invited to their homes and attended special events together. Then as age increased the differences between the values of our children and their friends, their attraction to each other decreased. I remember the night one daughter returned home early from an end-of-the-season athletic team party at which many of her friends were drinking alcoholic beverages and some were passed out on the floor. I could see the hurt in her eyes as she realized the moral gulf that now existed between her and her teammates. One of the outcomes of these changes in values has been that our children have become each other's best friends.

Another way we judge ourselves by our attractions is by where we want to be and what we want to do. In the same way that those with similar spiritual natures are drawn to each other, they are also attracted to similar spiritual environments consistent with their natures. Instead of climatic zones characterized by rainfall and temperature, spiritual environments are classified by kingdoms and laws. The Lord revealed to the Prophet Joseph Smith that those with similar spiritual natures will obey the same laws and dwell together in similar kingdoms. Elder James E. Talmage explained: "It is evident that the final judgment of mankind is to be reserved until after the resurrection; while in another sense judgment is manifest in the segregation of the disembodied, for in the intermediate state, like will seek like, the clean and good finding companionship with their kind, and the wicked congregating through the natural attraction of evil for evil."[2]

To abide in the celestial kingdom, one must abide the celestial law. To abide in the terrestrial kingdom, one must abide the terrestrial law (D&C 88:21–22, 37). Obedience to laws is a reflection of what attracts one's thoughts and desires. Those who choose to obey celestial laws do so because their thoughts and desires are celestial. Those who obey terrestrial laws do so because their thoughts and desires are terrestrial. The Lord's people inherit the kingdom where God dwells because their thoughts, desires, and actions are like those of the Savior. The Lord's people experience feelings of intense joy and happiness because they live in accordance with the celestial law to which they are attracted.

Because of the principle of attraction, it is likely that we create earthly homes that resemble the kingdom to which we will be drawn in the hereafter. If we create homes of happiness and service here, we will likely be drawn to the same home in the hereafter. If we are drawn to homes of discouragement and conflict here, we will be drawn to the same home in the hereafter. Thus, the earthly homes that we help create will be a foreshadowing of our heavenly homes we later inherit.

The wonderful truth about our earthly homes is that they can become corners of heaven on earth by following principles established by our Father in Heaven for that purpose. President Ezra Taft Benson taught: "If you will follow the admonitions of the Lord and heed the counsel of His chosen servants in their callings as prophets, seers and revelators, I promise you that love at home and obedience to parents will increase; faith will be developed in the hearts of the youth of Israel and they will gain power and strength to combat the evil influences and temptation which beset them. Each of our homes may veritably become a little heaven on earth."[3]

The parable of the prodigal son is an interesting case study in attraction. After following his father's life style for a number of years, he yearned for what he had never experienced. So he cashed out his inheritance to search for something that doesn't exist: happiness that does not require obedience to gospel principles. He assumed that he could buy happiness—and invested all his worldly wealth to find it. We cannot doubt that his natural man found pleasure from his riotous living. But that pleasure lasted only as long as his money. Then came the realization that he had exhausted his fortune without finding the happiness that lasts.

It is hard to imagine what the prodigal son's attractions were at the end of his excesses. He experienced hunger and debasement and longed for a better meal. These he one time enjoyed but were now denied him. He must have also longed for the love and respect he had one time enjoyed at his home that were now absent in his life.

Some say that fish are the last to discover water. Others say that fish never will discover water unless they are removed from it. Is it possible that we and the prodigal son are a little like the fish? The prodigal son needed to be denied the blessings of a caring family and a home-cooked meal before he recognized them as blessings. Perhaps all of us needed to have an earth life experience separated from the presence of our Father in Heaven to fully develop the attraction to return. Then one day after our journey through earth life is over, we will come to fully appreciate that secret something that calls us to our former home in heaven.

The Principle of Attraction and Our Judgments of Others

There is an important connection between the principle of attraction and the judgments we make of others. Because we are drawn to those similar to ourselves, we tend to assume that others are just like us. If the principle of restoration implies that we harvest what we sow, the principle of attraction implies that we judge the harvest of others by what we have planted.

The Book of Mormon illustrates how the principle of attraction directs our judgments of others. Laman and Lemuel said of Nephi: "he has thought to make himself a king and a ruler over us, that he may do with us according to his will and pleasure" (1 Nephi 16:38). To this complaint, Lehi responded: "ye have accused him that he sought power and authority over you; but I know that he hath not sought for power nor authority over you, but he hath sought the glory of God, and your own eternal welfare" (2 Nephi 1:25).

It was not Nephi who wanted to be a ruler over his brothers, but Laman and Lemuel who sought to selfishly subjugate Lehi's family. Later this same disgruntled duo complained that Nephi had been angry with them. To this judgment, Lehi responded: "Ye say that he hath used sharpness; ye say that he hath been angry with you; but behold, his sharpness was the sharpness of the power of the word of God, which was in him; and that which ye call anger was the truth, according to that which is in God, which he could not restrain, manifesting boldly concerning your iniquities" (2 Nephi 1:26).

Laman and Lemuel's guilty consciences pricked them as they observed their righteous brother. They judged Nephi's harvest of good deeds by the bitter seeds of selfishness they had planted. As a result, they assumed his desires were their own. Similarly, the principle of attraction may often lead us to assume our personal motives to be those of others. One of my high school friends reflected this application of the principle of attraction with the couplet: the faults we look for in others are often the ones we possess ourselves.

I experienced first-hand how one's own point of view colors one's perception of the actions of others. In 1974, my family and I were watching the Christmas parade in our Texas community of Bryan–College Station. I was holding our then two-year-old daughter Lana in my arms so she could better view the floats and other parade entries. Like most parades, this one had its share of office holders taking advantage of the opportunity to meet the voters. One burly, bearded politician riding in the parade passed our daughter and lifted up his two fingers, the signal of love and peace and opposition to the Viet Nam War. In response to his two finger signal, our daughter Lana lifted up her two fingers and declared: "Two? I'm two, too."

For our two-year-old daughter, the only reason one would lift two fingers in the air would be to declare one's age. She was convinced that the burly, bearded man was declaring his age. Just as our two-year-old daughter judged the behavior of others from her own perspective—so we frequently judge the harvest of others based on what we have planted.[4]

The Lesson

Persons with similar traits attract and often judge each other from the perspective of their own motives. The peace and happiness of a righteous people follows from their keeping company with the Holy Ghost, which leaves them attracted to the good and kind and finding virtues in all they meet.

Chapter Five

5 – The Principle of Conformity: As with the Priest, so with the People

❧

The principle. The principle of conformity is this: *when and where* the leader leads, *then and there* the people follow. Isaiah described the principle of conformity when he noted the important influence of leaders. He wrote: "as with the people, so with the priest" (Isaiah 24:2). Ezekiel added: "As is the mother, so is her daughter" (Ezekiel 16:44). Applications of the principle of conformity include: As with the parents, so with the children; as with the teacher, so with the students; and, as with the bishop, so with the ward. Acknowledging the importance of leaders, a famous general declared that he would prefer an army of mules lead by a lion than an army of lions led by a mule.

The tendency of the people to conform to their leaders suggests that we must choose our leaders and companions carefully. Recognizing that people tend to adopt the characteristics of those with whom they associate, we read in Proverbs: "make no friendship with an angry man; and with a furious man thou shalt not go: Lest thou learn his ways, and get a snare to thy soul" (Proverbs 22:24–25). President Gordon B. Hinckley has warned of our tendency to take on the ways of the world. He said: "We don't adopt them immediately, but we slowly take them on, unfortunately."[1]

The principle of conformity explains that conflict between the people and their leader is an unnatural state that is often resolved when the people adopt the qualities of their leaders. Wicked leaders who, like the devil, desire all men to be miserable like themselves, often lead their people to adopt some undesirable qualities (2 Nephi 2:18, 27). In this instance we acknowledge the principle of conformity by declaring that: "a rotten apple spoils the barrel." Great disasters in human history occurred when rotten apples such as Hitler, Nehor, Korihor, and wicked king Noah spoiled the barrel.

Fortunately, positive qualities can be shared just as well as negative ones. So when the people conform to the desirable qualities of their leaders we declare that "a little honey sweetens the pot." Consider the influence of two great leaders, Winston Churchill and chief captain Moroni, who sweetened the pot and stiffened the spines of those they led.

Isaiah Berlin wrote that during the German bombing blitz on London, Churchill was able with his stirring speeches to will British courage into existence by getting his compatriots to see themselves in the same, almost mythic terms in which he saw them. This allowed London to endure the blitzkrieg unblinking. It kept the pilots in the air long past the point of exhaustion. In the end, it changed the outcome of the war.[2]

In the case of Moroni, it was recorded that during a critical battle between the Nephites and Lamanites:

[T]hat the men of Moroni saw the fierceness and the anger of the Lamanites, [and] they were about to shrink and flee from them. And Moroni, perceiving their intent, sent forth and inspired their hearts with these thoughts—yea, the thoughts of their lands, their liberty, yea, their freedom from bondage.

And it came to pass that they turned upon the Lamanites, and they cried with one voice unto the Lord their God, for their liberty and their freedom from bondage.

And they began to stand against the Lamanites with power (Alma 43:48–50).

The courage and determination of Winston Churchill and chief captain Moroni were in conflict with weak thoughts and cowardly deeds. Their strong examples and the principle of conformity willed into existence the strength and determination of their people.

The principle of conformity may have led Paul to teach that those intending to marry should find a conforming companion. "Be ye not unequally yoked together with unbelievers" (2 Corinthians 6:14). President Spencer W. Kimball emphasized the need for conformity between marriage partners when he taught that religious differences imply wider areas of conflict, often leading to conflicting loyalties between church and family. President Kimball also taught that, without a common faith, trouble lies ahead for the marriage regardless of the other areas of conformity. There are some exceptions, he taught, but the rule is a harsh and unhappy one.[3]

The principle of conformity also explains the power of peer pressure. Feeling the need for acceptance, we often conform to the standards of others rather than risk separation and exclusion. Peer pressure is especially strong among the youth. I remember teaching one early morning seminary class in which all but one of the young men in the class arrived wearing their baseball hats backwards. Peer pressure had repositioned their hats. The crowd's adoption of bell bottom trousers, paisley ties, hula hoops, tie-dyed shirts, shagged hair, flapper shirts, blue suede shoes, rolled bobby socks, Volkswagen Bugs, words like "cool", "groovy", "far out", and "no way", fins on cars, mini skirts and knee length boots, pet rocks, and love beads all exemplify the principle of conformity at work.

Some instances of conformity are harmless and in many cases may be helpful such as when everyone agrees to drive the speed limit and stop at red lights. However, in matters relating to the spirit, the world has proven to be a reckless trend setter.

Goal Setting and the Principle of Conformity

Someone once described goal setting as planned conflict. A goal is a challenge to the status quo. It is an assault on our current comfort zones. Goals can be important in our progress because the conflict created by goals requires we respond by conforming to our goals or abandoning them for other standards. Without the conflict created by setting goals, we would most likely continue in our current course without giving much thought to a change in our direction, as long as it was comfortable.

Understanding why change requires conflict helps us to understand why tests created by opposing forces are such an important part of this life's experiences. It is only by creating a healthy state of discomfort that we become interested in change. The strength of this conflict is a major factor in determining the likelihood of our achieving our goals because the lack of conformity will drive us to conform to our desired goals or abandon them.

On at least two occasions, the Lord changed the lives of men by creating a significant conflict in their lives in presenting them with a new leader. To the Apostle Paul, the resurrected Lord appeared and asked: "Saul, Saul, why persecuteth thou me?" When Paul recognized the significant lack of conformity between what he was doing and the will of the Lord whom he desired to serve, his life was forever changed as he followed and conformed to a new leader. Likewise, Alma the Younger changed his life forever when an angel appeared to him and he realized the enormity of his sins. He, like Saul, found a new leader.

Worship and the Principle of Conformity

To worship is to esteem or reverence someone or something. We worship God by paying Him divine honors.[4] Zenos equated worship to prayer through which we express our reverence for God. In a more general sense, we worship what we consider to be our ultimate good.

Our ultimate good becomes our God. To worship God is to acknowledge His goodness and to desire to become like him. By recognizing an object or person worthy of worship, we are led naturally to ask: what is different between me and what I worship? Then, the principle of conformity directs our actions and efforts into becoming like what we worship. When we worship God, we seek to resolve differences between His example and our lives.

God, through Moses, taught the importance of carefully choosing the object of our adoration. "Thou shalt have none other gods before me" (Deuteronomy 5:7). Then God gave additional instruction on proper worship. He commanded: "Thou shalt not make thee any graven image, or any likeness of any thing that is in heaven above, or that is in the earth beneath, or that is in the waters beneath the earth" (Deuteronomy 5:8). Why? Because there will be a tendency to worship them instead of the true and living God. The Hebrew translation of this last verse adds insight about the consequence of our worship. In the Hebrew rendition of this scripture we read: "You shall not make yourself a graven image," that is, do not let your worship make you into less than a child of God.

The principle of conformity requires that we become what we worship. John, one of the Savior's Twelve Apostles, recorded that those who love the God of Israel and choose to conform their thoughts, feelings, and actions to His, will become like him. "Beloved, now are we the sons of God, and it doth not yet appear what we shall be: but we know that, when he shall appear, we shall be like him; for we shall see him as he is" (1 John 3:2). Finally, to the Prophet Joseph Smith the Lord revealed:

> They who dwell in his presence are the church of the Firstborn; and they see as they are seen, and know as they are known, having received of his fulness and of his grace;
>
> And he makes them equal in power, and in might, and in dominion. [D&C 76:94–95]

Alma, the son of Alma, who experienced a mighty change in his thoughts, desires, and deeds, described the consequences of conforming oneself to Christ's image. He asked: "And now behold, I ask of you, my brethren of the church, have ye spiritually been born of God? Have ye received his image in your countenances? Have ye experienced this mighty change in your hearts?" (Alma 5:14).

A spiritual rebirth requires that our hearts are changed so that our desires are like those of the Savior's. It means our deeds are patterned after His righteous works. Then, those who observe the changes in us will see a new countenance. Part of the rebirth involves receiving a gift, namely, the gift of charity. We are encouraged by the scriptures to pray for the gift of charity because charity reflects the nature of God. The blessing promised to us if we live worthy and acquire the gift of charity is that when we see God we will be like him.

> Wherefore, my beloved brethren, pray unto the Father with all the energy of heart, that ye may be filled with this love, which he hath bestowed upon all who are true followers of his Son, Jesus Christ; that ye may become the sons of God; that when he shall appear we shall be like him, for we shall see him as he is; that we may have this hope; that we be purified even as he is pure. Amen. [Moroni 7:48]

Expectations and the Principle of Conformity

The principle of conformity suggests that parents' expectations play a critical role in setting the standard to which their children will conform. As a young boy I once overheard my mother compliment my ability to rake leaves to a visiting neighbor. Since that day I have been a meticulous leaf raker, confirming my mother's expectation that became my own.

The expectations of parents may not always lead their children to lofty achievements. Some time ago my wife, Bonnie, observed a harried mother in a busy airport. The mother, apparently worried about losing control of her two small children on the crowded concourses, put leashes on her children. This was not strange. Other parents had resorted to this method of restraining their children before. What did appear strange was that the two small children were on their hands and knees barking and in other ways acting like dogs. These children were simply meeting their mother's expectation. When she put them on leases like dogs, they reasoned that their mother expected them to act like dogs.

A member of our stake presidency once shared with me an experience that he said occurred repeatedly. During a visit to a ward he would meet a parent and comment on the great potential of his or her child. He reported that most often and in the presence of the child, the parent would respond with a criticism of the child. The principle of conformity suggests that criticism of this nature would set a low standard for the children to conform, much like the children who were conforming to the behavior of canines.

An interesting study was conducted in an elementary school. Teachers in two different classrooms with students of the same age and equal ability were given different messages about their students. In the one class, the teacher was told her students were high achievers and would excel in their studies. The second teacher was told her students were remedial and would likely require extra effort to obtain ordinary results. At the end of the year, test scores across all subjects were consistently higher in the classroom in which the teacher had high expectations for her students.[5] Fortunately, the gospel of Jesus Christ plants in our hearts high expectations. The apostle Peter declared: "ye are a chosen generation, a royal priesthood, an holy nation, a peculiar people; that ye should shew forth the praises of him who hath called you out of darkness into his marvellous light" (1 Peter 2:9).

The Principle of Restoration and Conformity

The principle of conformity is a special application of the principle of restoration. The principle of restoration declares that that which we do send out shall return and be restored. The principle of conformity declares that how one leads will be returned in the lives of those who follow. Thus, the examples of the priests and parents will be returned to them in the lives of those they lead.

I one time learned about the principle of conformity when serving as a counselor in the stake presidency. At the time our stake was purchasing a stake farm to be paid for through ward budget assessments. The stake president assigned me to work with the wards and branches in our stake to help raise the necessary funds. In that assignment I learned an important lesson. In those wards and branches where the bishops and branch presidents were personally contributing to the purchase of the stake farm, the ward and branch members did also. In those few cases where the ward leaders were not supporting personally the purchase, neither was the ward.

President Boyd K. Packer once described an application of the principle of conformity applied to the priest. He described a visit he once had with a bishops' council. He asked them what were some of their most difficult problems? One of the bishops responded that in his ward, members were reluctant to accept callings. President Packer then said, noting the congeniality of the council, "Bishop, I know something else about you. You're not a good follower, are you? Aren't you the one who is always questioning what the stake president asks of his bishops?" The other bishops in the room started to chuckle and nodded their heads—he was the one.[6] It appears that as it is with the bishop, so it is with the members.

Internal Conformity

We have described the principle of conformity as it exists between leaders and those led. But there is another kind of conformity to which the principle of conformity applies. The conformity is between our two selves. On the one hand, "man is spirit" (D&C 93:33), an offspring of Deity with unlimited eternal possibilities. On the other hand, man is housed in flesh and is subject to physical desires, appetites, and passions.[7] The spirit and the body constitute the soul of man (see D&C 88:15), and it is the redemption of the soul, not just the body, that is God's work and glory.

Sometimes this physical being is referred to as the natural man who, if not disciplined, acts like a toddler. The toddler, like the natural man, is overly sensitive to physical stimulus, has difficulty postponing the gratification of his desires, and fails to see far-away consequences of his or her choices. Fortunately, we have another being capable of disciplining our toddler: our spirit. The spirit learns through different mechanisms than does the body. The spirit learns by receiving inspiration from the Almighty and the light of Christ that gives light to every man that cometh into the world (D&C 84:46). The ordinance of confirmation bestows on each worthy person the gift of the Holy Ghost through which angels may speak and through which power we may know the truth of all things (2 Nephi 32:3, Moroni 10:5).

The question that we each answer as we exercise our agency is: who leads us? Are we led by our toddler or our spirit? If our spiritual nature leads, then we turn naturally to the prompting of the Holy Ghost. But if our toddler leads and we ignore the prompting of the Holy Ghost, then the influence of the Holy Ghost leaves and we are left to our physical selves. This internal application of the principle of conformity was well summarized in a play written by Shakespeare.

In the play *Hamlet,* Shakespeare has his character Polonius say to his Laertes, "This above all: to thine own self be true, And it must follow, as the night the day, Thou canst not then be false to any man."[8] I understand this line from Shakespeare to mean that our real self to which we must be true, is our spiritual nature and being true to our own self, means yielding "to the enticings of the Holy Spirit."

Joseph Smith describes the process of being true to one's spiritual self and the conformity that follows.

> A person may profit by noticing the first intimation of the spirit of revelation; for instance, when you feel pure intelligence flowing into you, it may give you sudden strokes of ideas, so that by noticing it, you may find it fulfilled the same day or soon; . . . those things that were presented unto your minds by the Spirit of God, will come to pass; and thus by learning the Spirit of God and understanding it, you may grow into the principle of revelation, until you become perfect in Christ Jesus.[9]

Our spirits may direct conformity to our Christlike selves by instructing our minds to believe what the Lord has taught. President Packer counseled: "The flow of revelation depends on your faith. You exercise faith by causing, or by making, your mind accept or believe as truth that which you cannot, by reasons alone, prove for certainty."[10]

Each of us will face internal conflicts as our spirit and our toddler vie for control. The conflict between our spirit and our toddler will likely begin on the battlefield of our thoughts. Temptations originate with a thought. Our thoughts are the spiritual mothers of our desires and our acts. President David O. McKay declared: "The thought always precedes the act."[11]

If we resist temptation and put evil thoughts out of our minds, the principle of conformity means that the temptation must leave as well. President David O. McKay taught that Satan tempts us in our weakest areas and that if we resist his temptations, we will gain strength. Then Satan will tempt us in another point, and if we resist, he becomes weaker, and we become stronger.[12] Richard L. Evans wrote that opportunities to do evil and to do good are everywhere, but we shouldn't tempt temptation. Elder Evans continued. "When some people flee from temptation, they leave a forwarding address. If we don't want temptation to follow us, we shouldn't act as if we are interested."[13] Changing our spiritual address may require changing our companions; it may also require changing what we read and study; it also means changing our thoughts from the world to focusing on the Savior.

Some popular psychologist may teach the doctrine that man is like a stimulated toddler who naturally must respond, like Pavlov's dog, by salivating at each ring of the bell. But the gospel teaches that between the stimulus and the response is an exercise of will. It is the exercise of this will, a struggle for leadership between our toddler and our spirit, which leads us to righteousness or slavery depending on whom we choose for our leader.

Because sin is initially in conflict with our spiritual natures, Satan introduces it gradually. A familiar folk tale is that a frog will fail to hop out of a boiling pot if the temperature has been increased very slowly. The principle is that if the frog is allowed to gradually adjust to the changes in temperature, the conflict between the desired and actual water temperature will not be enough to motivate the frog to take action. A couplet by Alexander Pope describes the gradual process Satan uses to lead us to conform to his standards.

> Vice is a monster of so frightful mien,
> As to be hated needs but to be seen;
> Yet seen too oft, familiar with her face,
> We first endure, then pity then embrace.[14]

Gradualism and the frogs may explain why those who have done good and those who have failed to do good don't always know it. Those who had chosen to serve asked: "when saw we thee an hungered, and fed thee? Or thirsty, and gave thee drink? When saw we thee a stranger, and took thee in? Or naked, and clothed thee? Or when saw we thee sick, or in prison, and came unto thee?" (Matthew 25:37–39).

We all develop through our choices, thoughts, and desires controlling habits with which we are comfortable. And we, like those who served the Savior, may be surprised at our habits because they require so little effort to be maintained. In addition, the principle of attraction predicts that change is often difficult, and big changes are more difficult than little changes. As a result, when we progress it is likely to be line upon line; here a little and there a little. For most of us, the equilibrium level of our thoughts, actions, and desires changes slowly.

Sin and the Impossibility of Internal Conformity

The principle of conformity applied to the conflict between our toddler and our spiritual self predicts that we eventually must choose one of the two masters to serve. Satan tempts the toddler; the Savior seeks to elevate the spirit. Our spiritual progress toward Godhood requires our willingness to conform to His spiritual desires. Sin is the evidence of conformity to our carnal desires. It places us in conflict between what we know is right and what we do. The discomfort created by acting in conflict with our knowledge of right and wrong was described in Proverbs:

> Can a man take fire in his bosom, and his clothes not be burned?
>
> Can one go upon hot coals, and his feet not be burned?
>
> So he that goeth into his neighbor's wife; whosoever toucheth her shall not be innocent.
>
> But whoso committeth adultery with a woman lacketh understanding: he that doeth it destroyeth his own soul. [Proverbs 6:27–29, 32]

If we let our physical desires rule, then we create an unresolvable conflict. The conflict is between our spiritual nature enlivened by the spirit of Christ and our physical desires that lead us to gratify our passions and vain ambitions. The spirit of the Lord cannot dwell in an unclean temple. So when we sin, the spirit of the Lord is grieved and leaves. Yet we depend on the spirit of the Lord to sustain our spirits because we are spirit children of our Heavenly Father. So, in effect, sin creates spiritual orphans always looking for their home. Alma taught his son, Corianton, that sin could never create happiness because it is in conflict with our divine natures (Alma 41:10–11). Moroni taught the same lesson, that iniquity chases away hope, a precursor to happiness: "And if ye have no hope ye must needs be in despair; and despair cometh because of iniquity" (Moroni 10:22).

Often, men and women experience physical consequences from sin because their spirits are afflicted by a lack of conformity with righteousness. Zeezrom sinned and suffered spiritually and physically. The scriptures record: "And also Zeezrom lay sick at Sidom, with a burning fever, which was caused by the great tribulations of his mind on account of his wickedness, for he supposed that Alma and Amulek were no more; and he supposed that they had been slain because of his iniquity. And this great sin, and his many other sins, did harrow up his mind until it did become exceedingly sore, having no deliverance; therefore he began to be scorched with a burning heat" (Alma 15:3–4).

C. S. Lewis described how our natures require that we obey God if we are to find peace.

> [Some] seek to invent some sort of happiness for themselves without God. And out of that hopeless attempt has come nearly all that we call human history—money, poverty, ambition, war, prostitution, classes, slavery—the long terrible story of people trying to find something other than God which will make them happy. The reason why it can never succeed is this. God made us: invented us as a man invents an engine. A car is made to run on gasoline, and it would not run properly on anything else. Now God designed the human machine to run on Himself. He Himself is the fuel our spirits were designed to burn, or the food our spirits were designed to feed on. There is no other. That is why it is just no good asking God to make us happy in our own way without bothering about religion. God cannot give us a happiness and peace apart from Himself, because it is not there. There is no such thing.[15]

C. S. Lewis recognized the fundamental truth determining the principle of conformity. We are children of our Father in Heaven and we have a divine potential. We can find joy in the realization of our potential, or unhappiness in our failure to subdue the natural man and woman.

The Lesson

I had the privilege on two occasions to travel with Elder Spencer W. Kimball. The first occasion was when Ecuador was opened to missionary work. Along with our mission president, J. Avril Jesperson, and Elder Franklin D. Richards, my three companions and I spent some days never to be forgotten visiting cities in Ecuador and planning our proselytizing efforts. On our last day together we drove to the top of a mountain in downtown Quito and listened to a prophet dedicate the land of Ecuador for the preaching of the gospel and felt the Lord's presence there. On a later occasion I accompanied Elder Kimball during his tour of parts of Bolivia. During this tour, I translated his talks into Spanish and translated the talks of members from Spanish into English so that Elder Kimball could understand their messages.

I knew then that I was in the presence of a prophet of God. He was the most gentle and considerate man I have ever known. He treated me and everyone he met with love and respect. He radiated goodness that I knew came from his humble dependence on God. I will ever be grateful for the privilege of seeing Christlike qualities demonstrated by one who placed his trust in God. I have been forever changed as a result of those two experiences. He represented what I wanted my life to become. I could see that in following the Savior and striving to do His will, Elder Kimball had indeed become more like the Savior whom he worshiped. His example gave me hope that I could also become like the Holy One of Israel if I too would worship the true and living God.

I believe our Heavenly Father's greatest desire is for His children to return to His presence following their period of testing. I also believe that He knows that we would not be comfortable in His pure presence unless we have conformed to His qualities.

6 – The Principle of Separation: A House Divided

❦

The principle. The principle of separation teaches: *if* the leaders and the people cannot conform by adopting each other's qualities *then* they will separate, often physically and always emotionally. The Savior provided the scriptural foundation for this principle in what has become a familiar slogan. "And Jesus knew their thoughts, and said unto them, Every kingdom divided against itself is brought to desolation; and every city or house divided against itself shall not stand" (Matthew 12:25). On another occasion the Lord taught the principle of separation when He declared: "no man can serve two masters. He will either hate the one and love the other; or else he will hold to the one and despise the other" (Matthew 6:24).

One time travelling in the East with my family, we became lost and needed directions. The first place we found to ask for directions was a combination bar and grill. I stopped our car and asked my family to wait while I went inside. I entered a dark room where several men were seated at a bar and a few others were playing pool. The men eyed me suspiciously. I asked one of the men seated at the bar how I could get back to the main highway. Another one of the men seated at the bar made some mocking remark and some of the other men laughed at my expense. Fortunately, the man I asked gave me directions and I quickly left. I felt a great relief once I was back with my family and on the road. My discomfort in the bar and grill and my desire to leave can be explained by the principle of separation.

Abraham Lincoln used the Savior's teaching about the instability of a divided house to describe the inevitable outcome of the conflict over slavery between the Southern and Northern states. He prophesied in his famous house divided speech that the nation could not long endure half slave and half free. His prophecy was fulfilled with awful fury. The Southern states chose to separate from the Union. The Northern states sought to prevent the Southern states from leaving. The eventual rebellion produced a bloodbath of brothers costing the lives of over five hundred thousand souls.

One reason people try to avoid conflict by separating is that conflict is painful. Conflict is a system out of equilibrium. Conflict cries out for consensus. Conflict cannot long be endured. Consider some well known conflicts that ended in separation.

The greatest conflict in the history of time occurred in our premortal state. The conflict was between Satan, the Son of the Morning and our Father in Heaven. In our premortal existence, the purposes of God the Father and Satan came into conflict. Satan's desires were selfish. The Father desired eternal life for His children (Moses 1:39), and when Satan failed to force his plan on mankind, he desired that all mankind be miserable like himself (2 Nephi 2:27). Conformity between the followers of our Father in Heaven and Satan was impossible. The inevitable consequence of this unresolvable conflict was the separation of Satan and his followers from our Father in Heaven and His faithful children.

Other well known separations include the following: Lot and Abraham separated to avoid a conflict over grazing rights. The children of Israel separated from the Egyptians so they could worship their own God and live free. Lehi and his family left Jerusalem because the people there would not repent. Later, Nephi and his followers separated from Laman and Lemuel and their followers because of a conflict over who was to rule. The American colonies separated politically from England over a conflict of taxation rights. Religious conflicts led the Saints in the latter days to separate from their neighbors in New York, Ohio, various locations in Missouri, and Illinois. From Christ's church, organized on a foundation of apostles and prophets, have separated and separated again thousands of Christian churches in conflict over doctrines and practices.

There are several ways to effect a separation. One way of separating is to eliminate or destroy one party to the conflict. Wars attempt this method of conflict resolution. Joseph and Hyrum were killed by an armed mob because the religion they revealed was in conflict with the established religions of their day. The Savior proposed a change in the religion of His day. His divinely inspired change was painful for many because it created a conflict between what was and what was right. The house of Israel divided over the Savior's teachings. The conflict could have been resolved through repentance and some did repent. But others choose to remove the one who originated the conflict—and, in the end, they crucified their King.

Sin and the Principle of Separation

Sin causes pain and discomfort because it places us in conflict with our divine self and the Savior. This conflict cries out for resolution. The scriptures describe four ways we respond to the conflict created by sin. We blame others, we deny we sinned, we lose hope, or we repent. These four conflict responses are well documented and each has its own identifying characteristics.

Blame others. The most frequent response to the conflict created by sin is to separate ourselves from the responsibility for the sin by blaming others. By declaring "it's not my fault" one attempts to shift the burden of one's sins to another. Laman and Lemuel had fine-tuned the art of blaming others for their sins. The scriptures record that they complained: "Our younger brother thinks to rule over us; and we have had much trial because of him; wherefore, now let us slay him, that we may not be afflicted more because of His words. For behold, we will not have him to be our ruler; for it belongs unto us, who are the elder brethren, to rule over this people" (2 Nephi 5:3).

It's difficult to feel sorry for Laman and Lemuel and their supposed afflictions at the hands of Nephi. They were the ones who beat Nephi with a rod, who bound him with strong cords until his legs and arms swelled, and who withheld their labor from the shipbuilding enterprise until rebuked by an angel. Yet this unrepentant, disgruntled duo still blamed Nephi. Unfortunately, the descendants of Laman and Lemuel kept the blaming tradition alive by continuing to blame others. Their descendants taught: "that they [the Lamanites] were driven out of the land of Jerusalem because of the iniquities of their fathers, and that were wronged in the wilderness by their brethren, and they were also wronged while crossing the sea;" (Mosiah 10:12).

I once visited an inactive member of the church. At one time this member had held a responsible position in the church. I asked him why he was inactive. His response was that a brother had cheated him in a business deal and as long as this brother held a leadership position in the church, he would not attend. Instead of accepting the responsibility to forgive others as we ask the Lord to forgive us, this brother preferred to blame another for his failure to keep the commandments.

Onetime, I overheard an argument between two of our children. One of them in exasperation responded to the other by saying: "you make me so mad!" What a convenient excuse for choosing an unrighteous emotion. You choose to be angry and then declare that someone else controls your choices. Of course, claiming that someone else controls our emotions denies the scripture: "Wherefore, the Lord God gave unto man that he should act for himself" (2 Nephi 2:16).

One telltale sign of an effort to blame others for one's sins is anger. Since telling a lie convincingly is hard to do, most rely on anger to improve their credibility. But since anger is not prompted by the Holy

Ghost, it must be recognized for what it is, a sham, a ruse, an act, an imposter, a deceitful effort to cover one's sins. Nephi warned: "wo unto all those who tremble, and are angry because of the truth of God! For behold, he that is built upon a sandy foundation trembleth lest he shall fall" (2 Nephi 28:28).

We cannot claim that our sins are someone else's responsibility. The gift of our agency opened the door for righteous acts and progress as well as for sin and backsliding. Furthermore, the principle of restoration ensures us that we cannot escape the consequences of our sins by blaming others. Instead, blaming others is a lie that increases the distance between us and our Savior that must be travelled to reach repentance.

It's not a sin. The second approach to resolving the discomfort between ourselves and divinity that is caused by sin is to declare that what we did was no sin. Satan and his followers suggested this approach. He taught, "lie a little, take the advantage of one because of his words, dig a pit for thy neighbor; there is no harm in this;" (2 Nephi 28:8).

In our efforts to disguise sin, the world has come to call evil good and good evil; put darkness for light and light for darkness; and put bitter for sweet and sweet for bitter (2 Nephi 15:20; Isaiah 5:20). Elder Neal A. Maxwell noted that as some people become harder, they use softer words to describe dark deeds. For example, abortion is now called "a reproductive health procedure" or "termination of pregnancy." Illegitimate births have been sanitized to become: "nonmarital birth" or "alternative parenting." Homosexual relationships are renamed "alternative life styles." Marital infidelity is renamed: "an expression of one's independence." Gambling is now "gaming." Calling a failed marriage a "no-fault divorce" makes it sound as if the separation just happened all by itself while the separated spouses were innocent bystanders. In the former Yugoslav Republic, genocide has been renamed "ethnic cleansing." Torture of prisoners has become "reeducation." Mothers abandoning children for the work place when no real material needs demand it are making a "career choice." And adultery and fornication are now considered natural and even healthy provided no unwanted pregnancy occurs.[1]

The conflict between ourselves and divinity, created by sin, cannot be healed by attempting to separate us from the sin by arguing there was no sin. Attempting still another lie, that what we did was no sin, adds still another conflict between ourselves and our divine potential and the Savior. The practice of correct principles rejects all politically correct efforts to call evil good and good evil.

There's no hope. A third unsuccessful approach to resolve the conflict between ourselves and divinity caused by sin is to abandon hope and cease to try for improvement (Moroni 10:21–22). One of our children came home from school one day dejected. I asked for an explanation for his depressed spirit. He told me that on this particular day he had encountered one disappointment and frustration after another. Included in his disappointing day were lower than expected exam scores, homework assignments that he couldn't do, and finally exclusion from a former circle of friends. He concluded from these experiences that he was simply a first class failure.

My response to him was: "Who would want you to believe that you are a failure?" He agreed that only Satan would want him to believe he lacked potential. Then we went to work on fixing some of his homework frustrations. Unfortunately, all too many of us believe that because of past sins we can never return home with glory, no matter what we do. We simply must replace despair with hope born of the Savior's promise that we are saved by grace after doing all that we can do.

When we abandon hope, we often strive to distance ourselves from divinity. Adam and Eve hid themselves after they broke God's commandment hoping to separate themselves from His presence.

Jonah tried to hide from his missionary responsibility to God. Some members today attempt to hide from the Lord at work or at places of diversion where they work and play rather than worship and reverence God. But where can we go and be separated from God or from the spark of divinity within us? From Him we cannot hide nor find separation.

Repentance. By exercising faith in the Atonement of Jesus Christ, repenting of our sins, and seeking for the blessings of the Holy Ghost, we can regain the comfort lost through the conflict between and sin and divinity. True conformity between our best selves and the Lord's spirit that dwells within us is the basis of the peace Christ promises to all who strive to conform their lives to His righteous example. Blaming others, assigning soft names to dark deeds, and descending into despair are Satan's way of creating a fatality out of a minor accident.

For those brief periods in which Laman and Lemuel stopped blaming Nephi and accepted their responsibility, they found peace. Nephi records that in those repentant moments, his brothers humbled themselves and even asked his forgiveness. What a different story we might read in the Book of Mormon if they had consistently accepted responsibility for their sins.

Consider the effect that repentance had on the afflicted Zeezrom. When Zeezrom learned that Alma and Amulek were in the land Sidon his heart began to take courage and sent for them. They came to Zeezrom and told him that because of Christ he could gain forgiveness of his sins and be healed from the conflict between himself and divinity. Zeezrom believed and was healed. The scriptures then record that: "Zeezrom leaped upon his feet, and began to walk; and this was done to the great astonishment of all the people" (Alma 15:11).

Finally, consider the effect on King Lamoni when he gave up his sins in response to the gospel message of Ammon. Describing the effect of King Lamoni's repentance, Mormon wrote: "[Ammon] knew that King Lamoni was under the power of God; he knew that the dark veil of unbelief was being cast away from his mind, and the light which did light up his mind, which was the light of the glory of God, which was a marvellous light of his goodness—yea, this light had infused such joy into his soul, the cloud of darkness having been dispelled, and that the light of everlasting life was lit up in his soul, yea, he knew that this had overcome his natural frame, and he was carried away in God" (Alma 19:6). The conflict between King Lamoni and divinity was settled.

Satan's substitutes for repentance, designed to reduce the discomfort caused by the conflict between sin and our divine nature, are summarized in the following verses.

> For behold, at that day shall he [Satan] rage in the hearts of the children of men, and stir them up to anger against that which is good [blame others].
>
> And others will he pacify, and lull them away into carnal security, that they will say: All is well in Zion; yea, Zion prospereth, all is well—[there is no sin]. [2 Nephi 28:20–21]

Blaming others, denying the sin, and abandoning hope of repentance lead only to continued misery and anxiety because one remains separated from his or her best self. Only our efforts to repent lead us to conformity with our divine potential and peace and happiness. When we humbly acknowledge our sins and shortcomings, we qualify for the balm of the Atonement—which is the only remedy from sin's discomfort.

The Ugly Duckling

The wonderful story of the ugly duckling teaches an important lesson about the principle of separation. Through some unusual circumstances, a baby swan found herself living the life of a dysfunctional duck. The ugly duckling was very unhappy because she was living a duck's life when she really was a beautiful swan. The ugly duckling experienced the conflict that always accompanies a lack of conformity. Her happiness came only when she discovered her true identity and joined her own kind.

The application of this story should be obvious. We can never find true joy living like a duck when we are indeed beautiful swans. We are not animals ruled by passions. We are not capitalists whose goal is to accumulate more material toys than our neighbors. We are not Satan's servants who must seek for the treasures of the world or the praise of men to feed our carnal desires. We are swans and eagles, children of God, created in His image and likeness, now living a little lower than the angels, but with wings of glory (D&C 20:18, Moses 6:8).

Because we are indeed children of God, we can never find comfort in creating conflicts between ourselves and divinity by yielding to the attractions of the ducks' world. We first must rediscover who we are, and then conform ourselves to the good and clean. A close friend of mine described the joy of finding conforming himself to his true identity.

My friend's parents were divorced when he was very young. His mother made his contact with his father and his father's family nearly impossible. She intercepted letters and gifts and left my friend to wonder why his father had abandoned him. Worse, my friend's mother lived a miserable life and left an unhappy legacy of childhood memories for my friend. Then my friend moved to a ward where priesthood leaders took an active interest in his welfare. One priesthood leader provided him employment and the other boys included him in their priesthood activities. My friend felt comfortable in this new environment. He began to feel like a swan. Later, he accepted a call to serve a mission and for the first time in his life visited his father's family in Salt Lake. These were all active and committed members of the church with strong testimonies. My friend told me of his first visit to his uncle's house and feeling the spiritual atmosphere there. He said to me, 'Being there I realized for the first time who I truly was. It was like trying on a glove that fit perfectly.'

During this period of mortality, we are allowed to choose for ourselves which kind of laws we will obey. In addition, we are placed in environments not of our choosing. For those saints living in telestial kingdom conditions not of their choosing, discomfort is likely. This is because their companions will find their examples unsettling. The Savior warned His disciples to expect this lack of acceptance of celestial conduct by members of the world. He prayed: "I have given them thy word; and the world hath hated them, because they are not of the world, even as I am not of the world" (John 17:14).

On occasions we may, like the ugly duckling, find ourselves in a climate we cannot control or easily exit. In such conditions, our only possibility is to change the conditions of the kingdom in which we reside. Joseph Smith was once arrested and placed in a "telestial" kingdom in which he was forced to listen to his cruel guards recount their abuses of the unarmed Saints, including women and children. Then suddenly, he rose to his feet and declared: "Silence ye fiends of the infernal pit. In the name of Jesus Christ I rebuke you, and command you to be still; I will not live another minute and hear such language. Cease such talk, or you or I die this instant!"[2] They ceased their vile talk.

Our power to conform ourselves to the good word of God and separate ourselves from the wickedness of the world was emphasized by the Lord in the "Tree of Life" vision presented to Nephi and Lehi. The river of waters represented the filthiness of the world. The rod of iron along the river represented the good word of God leading to the tree of life with its life saving and life enhancing fruit. In response to Laman and Lemuel's request for an interpretation of the dream, and particularly the river of water, Nephi responded:

And they said unto me: What meaneth the river of water which our father saw?

And I said unto them that the water which my father saw was filthiness; and so much was his mind swallowed up in other things that he beheld not the filthiness of the water. [1 Nephi 15:26–27]

The great plan of happiness allows us all to focus our mind and will on the things of God and to separate ourselves from the filthiness of the world even though we travel its path, eat its food, and pay our bills with its coins. Separating ourselves from the evil is one more way to find peace and happiness.

The Lesson

Sin separates us from our divine selves and the Savior and leaves us suffering. In this state of suffering, we find ourselves uncomfortable, unhappy, and sometimes in despair. Blaming others, becoming angry, denying the sin, and losing hope are Satan's unsuccessful substitutes for repentance. Only true repentance removes the suffering caused by sin and bridges the gap between our imperfect selves and our divine potential and the Savior. No matter how hard we try, Satan's substitutes will never heal a sin-stained heart. How thankful we all should be for our Savior's Atonement that has provided a sure means of relief from sin.

7 – Principle of Faith: Inflated "I" vs. Divine Dependence

❧

The principle. The principle of faith insists: *if* we have faith in the Lord Jesus Christ, *then* all righteous works are possible. The Savior taught the principle of faith to His disciples. He said: "If ye have faith as a grain of mustard seed, ye shall say unto this mountain, Remove hence to yonder place; and it shall remove; and nothing shall be impossible unto you" (Matthew 17:20). On another occasion, the Savior taught that all things are possible to "them that believe" (Mark 9:23). Nephi taught the same principle of faith to his doubting brothers. To them Nephi declared: "how is it that ye have forgotten that the Lord is able to do all things according to his will, for the children of men, if it so be that they exercise faith in him? Wherefore, let us be faithful to him" (1 Nephi 7:12).

Faith in the Lord Jesus Christ is the assurance that if we keep God's commandments we will receive His blessings. Faith in Jesus Christ leads us from hope in correct principles to actions that unlock the blessings and power contained in correct principles with promise. As a result of one's faith in Jesus Christ, a person can command the elements, heal the sick, or influence any number of circumstances when the occasion warrants. But perhaps the most important fruit of one's faith is to receive a forgiveness of one's sins.

When one has faith, that person has the assurance that through repentance and the Atonement of Jesus Christ and His resurrection, he or she can gain eternal life. Faith in Jesus Christ, the parent of so many good works, is built on a foundation of evidence of things hoped for but which are not seen (Hebrews 11:1; Moroni 7:41). An evidence that sustains our faith in the Savior is the witness of those who know. Elder Bruce R. McConkie wrote that: "Since . . . ordained to the holy apostleship, I have had but one desire—to testify of our Lord's divine Sonship and to teach, in purity and perfection, the truths of his everlasting gospel . . . from my earliest days [I] have known with absolute certainty of the truth and divinity of his great latter-day work."[1] Other evidence sustaining our faith in the Savior includes prophetic writings recorded in the scripture and the whisperings of the Holy Ghost confirming the Savior's divinity (Moroni 10:4). Finally, faith can be strengthened when one beholds in awesome wonder the works God's hands have made (Alma 30:44).

Faith and the Misplaced Focus on Self

All action is motivated by faith but not all faith is centered in Jesus Christ. Satan seeks to deceive mankind into misplacing his faith. The Apostle Paul warned: "Beware lest any man spoil you through philosophy and vain deceit, after the tradition of men, after the rudiments of the world, and not after Christ" (Colossians 2:8).

One worldly doctrine that leads to misplaced faith is the doctrine of the inflated "I," what President Boyd K. Packer refers to as the "I" problem. Elder Neal A. Maxwell refers to it as the problem of the spear-like vertical pronoun "I."[2] The doctrine of the "inflated I" was promoted by Korihor, who taught: ". . . there could be no atonement made for the sins of men, but every man fared in this life according to the management of the creature; therefore every man prospered according to his genius, and that every man conquered according to his strength; and whatsoever a man did was no crime" (Alma 30:17). President Gordon B. Hinckley is one whose faith in the Savior leads him naturally away from a focus on self. After reviewing a biography about himself by Sheri Dew, he lamented: "There is too much Gordon B. Hinckley in this book."[3]

The doctrine of the inflated "I" encourages its followers to replace their faith in the Savior with the worship of themselves. Thus, in the religion of the inflated "I", study of holy scriptures is replaced by preening in front of mirrors. It teaches that if we succeed, it's because we're smarter, stronger, and manage better than the rest—and we did it all by ourselves. Moreover, it leads us to believe that second place is for sissies.

Those who subscribe to the doctrine of the inflated "I" experience the following undesirable results. They are always learning and never coming to a knowledge of the truth (2 Timothy 3:7). They are always accumulating things of which they never have enough. They continually call attention to themselves and their achievements, but never receive adequate recognition for their efforts. They strive for self-actualization and improved self-esteem at the sacrifice of sanctification. They are oversensitive and easily offended by imagined or intended offenses. They must continually separate and elevate themselves from others since their frame of reference is the world. And if they suffer for their sins, they assume it is because of the shortcomings of others for which no repentance is required. Thus, those who follow the doctrine of the inflated "I" find in place of friends, competitors, and in place of communion, contests.

The most feared consequence of the inflated "I" is that it leaves us alone, the opposite of at-one-ment and joy. Because the doctrine of the inflated "I" defines success relative to what others do, its converts must adopt the goal of rising above the rest, being first in line, and having more than the rest. And if others have more, come in first, or have children more successful and beautiful than their own, they experience failure. To avoid second place, inflated "I" adherents will, if it is required to win, lie, deceive, steal, commit adultery, and take innocent life. At the end of the effort, however, is the disappointing discovery that in their effort to become number one, the inflated "I"s find themselves alone and lonely.

At the time of Pahoran, divisions among the people were over who had the most important genealogy (Alma 51:8). And in other times it was over who went to the finest schools, and wore the most expensive clothes (3 Nephi 6:12; 4 Nephi 1:24). Those who suffer from an inflated "I" are not choosy. They can use almost anything in the world to set themselves above and apart from the rest—for after all, being number one is their goal.

Daniel Judd, a Latter-day Saint psychologist, described a modern application of a misplaced focus on self:

> A few years ago while reading a magazine, I came across a cartoon that pictured a Catholic priest seated in the confessional giving counsel to a parishioner. On the shelves behind the priest and in his lap and hands were many of the "self-help" books we find in the psychology section of most bookstores. On a bottom shelf of the confessional booth rested the Bible . . . covered with cobwebs. The caption of the cartoon read: "Not to worry, my son, Get off your guilt trip and take the road less traveled. The good book says you're OK. All you need is to pull your own strings, focus on your erroneous zones, take control of your life, and self-actualize yourself so you can achieve your greatest potential . . . and you'll be just fine."[4]

I'm reminded of Brother Judd and his description of this cartoon when I hear members describe their problems or the problems of others as low self-esteem, a lack of self-confidence, inadequate amounts of self-love, failure to forgive oneself, or a poor self-image. One problem with defining our problems in the ways just described is that it leads us to ourselves. A second problem is that these self-diagnosed ailments are not identified in the scriptures as the real source of our sufferings. Thus, I must assume that our concern with self—self-love, self-image, and self-forgiveness is misplaced. And worse, this emphasis may be part of the philosophies of men mingled with and sometimes substituted for scripture that may lead to misplaced faith.

The Principle of Divine Dependence

In contrast to the doctrine of the Inflated "I," Ammon taught our dependence on divinity: "Yea I know that I am nothing; as to my strength I am weak; therefore I will not boast of myself, but I will boast of my God, for in his strength I can do all things; yea, behold, many mighty miracles we have wrought in this land, for which we will praise his name forever" (Alma 26:12).

The divine dependence doctrine is that we recognize that we are weak, but with God's help all things are possible. The divine dependence doctrine also acknowledges that God not only sends angels to strengthen and comfort us in our travels through our personalized Gethsemane, but also sends caring friends and family members, a compassionate counselor, and inspired priesthood leaders.

Consider some other examples of the divine dependence doctrine. The Savior taught His disciples:

> Which of you by taking thought can add one cubit unto his stature?
>
> And why take ye thought for raiment? Consider the lilies of the field how they grow; they toil not, neither do they spin;
>
> And yet I say unto you, that even Solomon, in all his glory, was not arrayed like one of these. [3 Nephi 13:27–29]

And Mormon notes:

> O how great is the nothingness of the children of men; yea, even they are less than the dust of the earth.
>
> For behold, the dust of the earth moveth hither and thither, to the dividing asunder, at the command of our great and everlasting God. [Helaman 12:7, 8]

The doctrine of divine dependence teaches us that divine support requires that we shift our focus from ourselves to our God. We read in the scriptures that Christ taught: "He that findeth his life shall lose it: and he that loseth his life for my sake shall find it" (Matthew 10:39). And elsewhere the Savior instructed:

> Take no thought for your life, what ye shall eat, or what ye shall drink; nor yet for your body, what ye shall put on. Is not the life more than meat, and the body than raiment? [Matthew 6:25]

> And whoso layeth down his life in my cause, for my name's sake, shall find it again, even life eternal. [D&C 98:13]

Depending on divinity does not imply that we are powerless or incapable of acting. Depending on divinity is just the opposite. We are bold and strong when in command of the powers of God, including the power to move mountains and raise families. Indeed, Joseph Smith taught that faith is a principle of power. The powers of God, however, in addition to faith require righteousness and thoughts garnished with virtue (D&C 121:45). Moreover, we who would exercise God's power must seek to do His work. Then after all that we can do is our effort finished with grace.

Nephi knew and understood the requirements for divine assistance and recorded:

> [T]he Lord spake unto me, saying: Blessed art thou, Nephi, because of thy faith, for thou hast sought me diligently, with lowliness of heart.

> And inasmuch as ye shall keep my commandments, ye shall prosper, and shall be led to a land of promise; yea, even a land which I have prepared for you; yea a land which is choice above all other lands. [1 Nephi 2:20–21]

Faith and the Principle of Restoration

The exercise of faith returns promised blessings to those who trust in the Lord and depend on Him for direction. In this sense the principle of faith, like other principles, is a special application of the principle of restoration. Some of the consequences of choosing to exercise faith in the Lord Jesus Christ are described next.

When we recognize our divine dependence, we are directed to our divine potential. If we focus on our selves, we may only discover the natural man or woman. Directing our attention to divinity may lead us to discover who we may become. In the Epistle of John we read: "And every man that hath this hope in him purifieth himself, even as he is pure" (1 John 3:3).

And in Psalms we are reminded of our divine creation:

> What is man, that thou art mindful of him? and the son of man, that thou visitest him?
>
> For thou hast made him a little lower than the angels, and hast crowned him with glory and honour.
>
> Thou madest him to have dominion over the works of thy hands; thou hast put all things under his feet: [Psalms 8:4–6]

When we recognize our divine dependence, we have a sure source of help. The world and the workers of wickedness will always abandon us in our time of need. God is our sure defense, a help in time of need, the living water in a dry desert, and the bread of life in a world starved for truth. To his son Shiblon, Alma taught: "And now my son, Shiblon, I would that ye should remember, that as much as ye shall put your trust in God even so much ye shall be delivered out of your trials, and your troubles, and your afflictions, and ye shall be lifted up at the last day" (Alma 38:5).

When we recognize our divine dependence, our confidence expands and our abilities and opportunities to do good are multiplied. Nephi reminded us that with divine assistance we can keep the commandments of God. Zeniff in his old age went to battle against the Lamanites because of the strength of the Lord (Mosiah 10:11).

It was because Mosiah recognized his divine dependence that he allowed his sons to serve a dangerous mission to the Lamanites. The Lord revealed to Mosiah: "Let them go up, for many shall believe on their words, and they shall have eternal life; and I will deliver thy sons out of the hands of the Lamanites" (Mosiah 28:7). Many more examples could be listed of the faithful being empowered by God to do many mighty deeds. What a relief it is to know that we aren't dependent on ourselves alone.

When we recognize our divine dependence, we recognize our infinite worth, not because we have improved our self-image, but because we more clearly understand our relationship to God, and take upon ourselves His image (Alma 5:14).

When we recognize our divine dependence, we realize that we can be cleansed from sin, saved, and exalted, even though we are not perfect. Alma the Younger described the experience of being cleansed from his sins.

> And it came to pass that as I was thus racked with torment, while I was harrowed up by the memory of my many sins, behold, I remembered also to have heard my father prophesy unto the people concerning the coming of one Jesus Christ, a Son of God, to atone for the sins of the world.
>
> Now, as my mind caught hold upon this thought, I cried within my heart: O Jesus, thou Son of God, have mercy on me, who am in the gall of bitterness, and am encircled about by the everlasting chains of death.
>
> And now, behold, when I thought this, I could remember my pains no more; yea, I was harrowed up by the memory of my sins no more.
>
> And oh, what joy, and what marvellous light I did behold; yea, my soul was filled with joy as exceeding as was my pain. [Alma 36:17–20]

Elder Bruce R. McConkie taught the comforting concept of exaltation without perfection through the Atonement of Jesus Christ. He testified: "everyone in the Church who is on the straight and narrow path, who is striving and struggling and desiring to do what is right, though is far from perfect in this life, if He passes out of this life while he's on the strait and narrow, he's going to go on to eternal reward in his Father's kingdom."[5]

When we recognize our divine dependence, we lose our fear of our fellow man. We no longer see them as competitors to be surpassed, but fellow citizens and friends. As our focus is changed from inflating our self-esteem to serving, our goal becomes to share and cooperate. Then, as the satisfaction from service spreads, a wonderful unity occurs and we find ourselves in Zion where we are of one heart, one mind, living righteously, and where there are no poor among us.

When we recognize our divine dependence, we are freed from the difficult duty of judging the world. With the burden of judgment lifted from us, we are free to be a friend and an advocate of the imperfect. I once interviewed a member of the Church who began our discussion saying: "I'm thinking of asking to have my name removed from the records of the Church." I asked why. This dear member then began a long recitation of the imperfections found in members of the Church. Those included in the list of the less than perfect were former missionary companions, a mission president, insensitive priesthood leaders, and less than diligent home teachers.

My response was: "I have wonderful news. You are now released from the difficult duty of seeing that justice is done in the lives of these less than perfect members. The Savior agreed to take that burden upon Himself and asks only that you forgive others so you can be forgiven" (see Mosiah 14:4). It's a wonderful relief to know that God is in His Heaven and will execute righteous judgments without our help (D&C 64:9–10).

Our divine dependence leads to one who has the directions we need to follow on our path toward perfection. The Savior's exemplary life is the perfect set of directions to obtain perfection and exaltation. Just as we might seek instruction from those skilled in the profession we wish to join, followers of Christ should learn about perfection from the one perfect man. We should learn to forgive as He forgave. We should share our substance with the poor as He fed the hungry thousands. We should pray to our Father in Heaven as He prayed. We should visit the temple as He did. We should share our testimony with those in spiritual darkness as He did. And we should care for our families as He did for His mother even while on the cross.

When we recognize our dependence, we are in condition to be born of the spirit. Alma, the son of Alma asked his people if they had spiritually been born of God. Or in other words, had they received the image of Christ in their countenances? "Have you," he asked, "experienced a mighty change in your hearts?" Divine dependence leads to a divine countenance and a pure heart, one that is changed and different from those who are not born of the spirit. Yet, the mighty change in our hearts cannot occur until we believe and acknowledge our dependence on God.

King Benjamin sent among his people to know if they believed the words which he had spoken unto them. His people all cried with one voice, saying: "Yea, we believe all the words which thou hast spoken unto us; and also, we know of their surety and truth, because of the Spirit of the Lord Omnipotent, which has wrought a might change in us, or in our hearts, that we have no more disposition to do evil, but to do good continually" (Mosiah 5:2). And then manifesting their changed disposition and divine views, the people responded: "And we, ourselves, also, through the infinite goodness of God, and the manifestations of his Spirit, have great views of that which is to come; and were it expedient, we could prophesy of all things" (Mosiah 5:3).

When we recognize our divine dependence, we develop attitudes of hope; that all things, including hard things, work together for good for those who love the Lord. To Joseph Smith, the Lord declared: "And if thou shouldst be cast into the pit, or into the hands of murderers, and the sentence of death passed upon thee; if thou be cast into the deep; if the billowing surges conspire against thee; if fierce winds become thine enemy; if the heavens gather blackness, and all the elements combine to hedge up the way; and above all, if the very jaws of hell shall gape open the mouth wide after thee, know thou my son that all these things shall give thee experience, and shall be for thy good" (D&C 122:7).

Divine dependence leads us to acknowledge that when hard things happen, with divine help, the experience can be used for good and to bless others. Christ suffered all things so that He could succor us in our times of need. Is it possible that sometimes we too must suffer atonement-like experiences so that we can comfort those in need of comfort and mourn with those who mourn?

Divine dependence leads us to the assurance of God's blessings. The most positive of attitudes that result from our recognizing our divine dependence is knowing that we can obtain the blessings God has promised to those who love and serve him. "What power shall stay the heavens? As well might man stretch forth his puny arm to stop the Missouri river in its decreed course, or to turn it up stream, as to hinder the Almighty from pouring down knowledge from heaven upon the heads of the Latter-day Saints" (D&C 121:33).

With this type of assurance, no wonder we should be the happiest people on earth.

Divine Dependence and Right Worship

Those with faith in God find their confidence while on their knees in prayer. Those who are determined to conquer according to their own strength may indeed achieve recognition and rewards from the worldly. Their pleasure, however, will one day be replaced by pathos when they realize how much they sacrificed in their efforts to be number one and alone.

To the faithful who trust God and strive to keep His commandments, Nephi promised: "And if it so be that the children of men keep the commandments of God he doth nourish them, and strengthen them, and provide means whereby they can accomplish the thing which he has commanded them; wherefore, he did provide means for us while we did sojourn in the wilderness" (1 Nephi 17:3).

Describing the lives of those who depend on God, President Ezra T. Benson wrote:

> Men and women who turn their lives to God will find out that He can make a lot more out of their lives than they can. He will deepen their joys, expand their vision, quicken their minds, strengthen their muscles, lift their spirits, multiply their blessings, increase their opportunities, comfort their souls, raise up friends, and pour out peace. Whosoever will lose his life to God will find he has eternal life.[6]

The principle of faith promises power to the worthy to move mountains. But what greater mountain is there for us to move than our own personal habits, attuned as they are to self-worship and worldly acquisitiveness? To move this mountain requires massive soul-moving equipment available only to those who depend on divinity. So we turn to God who is a mighty fortress, a tower of strength never failing. We recognize He is a helper mighty, who overcame all, and saved us from the fall. His might and power are great. He all things did create and He shall reign forevermore.[7]

The Lesson

In the musical pageant *The City of Joseph*, Joseph Smith explains that the things men believe in are the things men do. We express our faith in the Lord Jesus Christ by worshiping Him and obeying His commandments. Our faith in Christ leads us to do His work in His way.

Great changes occur in the lives of men and women who place their faith in God and realize that they are His children with the potential to become like Him. When those converted by Ammon's teachings acquired faith in Christ, they became brothers instead of belligerents. As a result of their realizing their dependence on God, they became like Him—and so can we.

Chapter Eight

8 – The Principle of Abundance: Overcoming Pride

ᥱᥩ

The principle. The principle of abundance assures us that *because* the earth is full *then* there is enough and plenty to share. The scriptural foundation for the principle of abundance is the Lord's declaration that "the earth is full, and there is enough and to spare; yea, I prepared all things, and have given unto the children of men to be agents unto themselves" (D&C 104:17).

The principle of abundance teaches that if there are shortages, the problem is not with the earth's resources but with man's unwillingness to share and work together. Adam Smith, the Scottish moral philosopher whose famous 1776 book *The Wealth of Nations* revolutionized economic thought, explained the value of working together. He observed that a pin maker working alone could scarcely produce one pin a day. But 10 men, Smith reported, working together could produce 48,000 pins in a day.[1] This increase in productivity was a result of specialization; when people specialize in a task, their ability to repeat the task increases. Moreover, specialization allows individuals to work at tasks for which they are most skilled.

Saints in Nauvoo gave further evidence of the benefits of working together. They divided the construction of wagons into specialized tasks and constructed over 2000 wagons during the winter of 1845 and 1846.[2] This was an incredible feat since one man skilled in wagon construction and working alone could hardly build one wagon every three months.

Amartya Sen, a recent winner of the Nobel Prize in economics, gave more evidence of the benefits of working together. He described the advantages of democratic governments whose people have the freedom to work together compared to controlled economies in which the people's freedom to work together is limited. Sen writes: "no famine has ever taken place in the history of the world in a functioning democracy—be it economically rich (as in contemporary Western Europe or North America) or relatively poor (as in post independence India, or Botswana, or Zimbabwe). Famines have tended to occur in colonial territories governed by rulers from elsewhere . . . or in one-party states, or in military dictatorships."[3]

The False Principle of Scarcity

It seems that for every true principle, there is a false alternative. In contrast to the principle of abundance is the false principle of scarcity. The scarcity principle teaches that *because* the earth is not full *then* there is not enough and none to share.

Those who believe in the principle of scarcity are convinced that only those who are fast or first in line will have enough at the end of the day. In other words, success depends on the management of the creature and what one does to win is no sin (Alma 30:17). Those who believe in the principle of scarcity live in fear of others who may be faster or first in line. Then fear eventually leads to resentment and enmity as the believers in scarcity come to view their problems as the creations of their neighbors. So belief in scarcity eventually converts neighbors into enemies and acquaintances into opponents. In contrast, faith in Jesus Christ and His abundance leads us to pure love that casts out all fear including the fear of our fellow man (Moroni 8:16).

Feelings of enmity are often equated to the sin of pride because the proud are concerned for their own well being without concern for others. The proud seek to be number one and to own the biggest share. The proud are boastful, puffed up because of their success, arrogant, past feeling, and rejoice in iniquity. The proud seek to separate themselves from others with their education, clothes, housing, cars, exclusive creeds, race, and employment. The proud are simply too busy to be bothered. The proud, in their quest for the praise of the world, need no friends, only admirers. As a result, small children who have not learned how to flatter without feeling, will never make the guest list of the proud.

President Ezra Taft Benson summarized the sin of pride. "Most of us think of pride as self-centeredness, conceit, boastfulness, arrogance, or haughtiness. All of these are elements of the sin, but the heart, or core, is still missing. The central feature of pride is enmity . . . enmity means 'hatred toward, hostility to or a state of opposition.' It is the power by which Satan wishes to reign over us. As he witnesses the destruction of his people, the prophet Mormon wrote to his son Moroni: 'Behold, the pride of this nation, or the people of the Nephites, hath proven their destruction except they should repent' (Moroni 8:27)."[4]

Those Who Believe in Scarcity

One thing must be said for the church of "scarcity," it has attracted an impressive list of members. In the premortal existence, Satan sought our Heavenly Father's glory at our expense. Apparently he believed that we could not all gain glory, so he proposed a plan in which he would win and we would lose. The Lord revealed to Joseph Smith: "for behold, the devil was before Adam, for he rebelled against me, saying, Give me thine honour, which is my power; and also a third part of the hosts of heaven turned he away from me because of their agency;" (D&C 29:36).

Cain saw the Lord's acceptance of Abel's offering as a threat to his own success. He believed the Lord's approval was limited and insufficient for both him and his brother Abel. As a result of his belief in scarcity, Cain rose up against Abel his brother, and slew him (Genesis 4:8).

Proud Laman and Lemuel believed that opportunities to lead were limited and when Nephi, because of his righteousness, was called to rule they sought to slay him. Other proud siblings sold their brother Joseph into Egypt because they thought their father could not love them all. Another brother saw the Prodigal Son's return as a threat to his own party plans and refused to welcome him home. Finally, the Pharisees, Scribes, and Sadducees saw the life-saving miracles of the Savior as a threat to their reserved seats in high places and plotted His destruction.

In a salute to scarcity, the Zoramites constructed a tower that they called the Rameumpton into which only one could enter. And in this exclusive tower they proudly prayed:

> we believe that thou hast elected us to be thy holy children; and also thou hast made it known unto us that there shall be no Christ.
>
> . . . and thou hast elected us that we shall be saved, whilst all around us are elected to be cast by thy wrath down to hell; for the which holiness, O God, we thank thee; and we also thank thee that thou hast elected us, that we may not be led away after the foolish traditions of our brethren, which doth bind them down to a belief of Christ, which doth lead their hearts to wander from thee, our God. [Alma 31:16–17]

A belief in scarcity sometimes leads us to withhold our tithes and offerings from the Lord and to be stingy with our time by refusing to accept callings. A concern for our scarce time sometimes keeps us from our home and visiting teaching assignments and sometimes requires us to work on the Sabbath to acquire those things which lack the ability to provide joy.

The Parable of the Diners

The difference between those who believe in scarcity or abundance is illustrated with the parable of the diners.

Consider a group of hungry diners seated at a banquet table on which is a single loaf of bread. The diners believe there is only one loaf of bread which is not enough for everyone to be filled. So because they believe in the scarcity of the bread supply, they fear that at the end of the meal, there will only be the quick and the hungry and they don't want to be hungry.

The diners' belief in the scarcity of the bread supply changes dinner table companions into competitors because their meal must come at the expense of others. In their competitive concern, each one seated at the table wonders what are the others planning and how they can be bested. And then, as the competitive diners think about the contest, they begin to resent and then to hate their table mates for threatening their success.

At another table across town sits another group of diners. They also face a single loaf of bread, recently baked and filling the room with a wonderful fragrance. The diners cheerfully share the loaf with each other because they know the chef. They know that he has a plentiful supply of bread and that he only places one loaf at a time on the table to keep the other loaves warm and fresh for the diners when additional bread is desired. These dinner companions are friends. They find no need to compete or rush their meal to ensure their share. Instead, they enjoy a pleasant dinner together.

In the first case, competition arose because the diners lacked confidence in the chef's ability to supply their needs. In the second case, cooperation and sharing occurred because the diners knew the chef and that he could and would supply their needs. And so it is with us. A lack of faith leads us to rely on our own strength and view others as competitors. In contrast, confidence in the Creator leads us to view our brothers as cooperators and friends.

Cooperation versus Competition

A belief in abundance sees the problem of a short supply to be a lack of cooperation and looks for ways to cooperate. A belief in scarcity sees the problem of short supply as too many competing for too few resources. For those who believe in scarcity, the solution is to compete for the biggest share, creating a spirit of competitiveness. But competition is a companion of pride. President Benson declared, "Pride is essentially competitive in nature. We pit our will against God's."

The dictionary defines competition as a struggle between rivals for a prize only one can possess. In other words scarcity, is required for competition. Thus the proud compete for a prize they can win only if another person loses. Referring to man's competitive nature that leads to pride the Lord declared to Joseph Smith: "He that exalteth himself shall be abased, and he that abaseth himself shall be exalted" (D&C 101:42). And to William W. Phelps the Lord spoke reprovingly: "he [Phelps] hath need to repent for I, the Lord, am not well pleased with him, for he seeketh to excel, and he is not sufficiently meek before me" (D&C 58:41). C. S. Lewis comes close to defining the essence of pride with its focus on competition when he wrote: "pride gets no glory out of having something, only having more of it than another."[5]

Connecting competition to pride and scarcity may be offensive to us at first. In the discipline of economics, competition is almost adored as the organizing engine that has produced wealth and prosperity in the Western world. Indeed, many of our activities are designed to produce competition by organizing them out of scarcity. In the game of musical chairs, competition is created by having fewer chairs than those that need them. Competition is created in sporting contests by having only one winning team or performer. Competition is created at the work place by having individuals compete for a single position. And more recently, we have transformed our courts into contests between expensive lawyers who sometimes emerge as the only winners.

Primary and Secondary Goods[6]

Our daughter Lana, after reviewing the above, wrote me the following. "But what if there really isn't enough bread? What if someone in the company must be let go? And what if at the end of the wrestling match there really is a winner and a loser?"

Then Lana shared with me the trying time she experienced in the Minneapolis Airport when her flight was cancelled and passengers jostled each other for the insufficient number of seats on the next plane out. She asked: how do we live in the real world where competition does exist and, if we don't compete, we may end up hungry at the end of the day?

I reflected on our daughter's comment and on the number of times (almost daily) that it appears we must compete for the single loaf of bread. It is true that unwillingness to share and mismanagement of our resources does create shortages out of abundance. There are famines and unemployment. But the message is that the problem is not with God's creation but with man's pride and unwillingness to share, attitudes that emerge when we believe in scarcity.

The issue our daughter raised is a problem of perspective. There are two kinds of goods—primary goods and secondary goods. Primary goods are the true sources of satisfaction. Secondary goods help us obtain primary goods. For example, the company of friends and family may be considered a primary good. The car in which we travel to be with friends and family is the secondary good. The Kingdom of God is a primary good—the world is a secondary good. Most mistakes in life occur when we confuse secondary goods for primary goods. This would be equivalent to focusing all of our attention on washing, waxing, and fueling our cars, but never using them to carry us to our destinations for fear of chipping the paint and dirtying the oil.

One example of mistaking primary goods for secondary goods occurred when the religious rulers at the time of Christ rebuked the Savior for healing on the Sabbath day. He reminded them that the Sabbath day was intended to turn their attention to Him and that the Sabbath day was made for man, not the other way around. The Sabbath day was a secondary good, Christ was the primary good.

Jacob taught the distinction between primary goods and secondary goods. He taught his people to seek first the kingdom of God, the primary good. Then he counseled, that they might seek riches but they would do so to feed the hungry and for other good reasons. In other words, once his people focused on the first good, the kingdom of God, their efforts to seek secondary goods would be for wise purposes (Jacob 2:18–19).

Brigham Young taught the need to distinguish between primary and secondary goods in the following passage. "I look around among the world of mankind and see them grabbing, scrambling, contending, and every one seeking to aggrandize himself, and to accomplish his own individual purposes, passing the community by, walking upon the heads of his neighbors—all are seeking, planning, contriving in their wakeful hours, and when asleep dreaming, 'How can I get the advantage of my neighbor? How can I spoil him, that I may ascend the ladder of fame?' This is entirely a mistaken idea . . . The man who seeks honour and glory at the expense of his fellow-men is not worthy of the society of the intelligent."[7]

My response to our daughter is that true saints seek their daily bread in the world for different reasons and guide their conduct with different rules than do those whose primary goals are to be first in line with the largest loaf of bread. To do otherwise is to confuse secondary goods for primary ones, to confuse the props of life's drama for the essence of life which is to progress to joy. I believe that when we distinguish between primary and secondary goods, we will become far less anxious about beating our neighbor, being at the head of the line, and winning wrestling matches because we recognize that success in the world is not equal to joy in the Kingdom.

President Spencer W. Kimball was once in a busy airport with crowed lines and used the opportunity to promote a primary good, the well being of a young mother with a small child. He politely asked those ahead of the mother in line if they would allow her to go ahead. They agreed and enjoyed a primary good in return.[8]

Scarcity of Time

Returning to the parable of the competitive diners, there is something more to be said of them. They not only saw the scarcity in the size of the loaf, but they also believed the time available for eating their bread to be limited. This scarcity of time view leads the competitive diners, and others who are proud, to focus on the here and now. Korihor taught the scarcity of time when he emphasized to his selfish students that when a man dies, that is the end (Alma 30:18). Those that believe in the scarcity of time, have no concern for what they believe is a nonexistent future. Nephi warned:

> and there shall be many which shall say: Eat, drink, and be merry, for tomorrow we die; and it shall be well with us.
>
> And there shall also be many which shall say; Eat, drink, and be merry; nevertheless, fear God—he will justify in committing a little sin; yea, lie a little, take advantage of one because of his words, dig a pit for thy neighbor; there is no harm in this; and do all these things, for tomorrow we die; and if it so be that we are guilty, God will beat us with a few stripes; and at last we shall be saved in the kingdom of God. [2 Nephi 28:7–8]

Translated, Nephi's warning is that Satan will teach that since there is no tomorrow, get all you can today.

An Unresolvable Conflict

The proud suffer an unresolvable conflict. They must compete against and be certified by the same worldly crowd. So at the same time the proud seek acceptance by those at the table, they must fight them for a bigger share of the loaf. The consequence of this unresolvable conflict among the competitive is divisions. In our parable of the competitive diners, there are two groups: the hungry and the hoarders. I say hoarders because all along there was enough bread for everyone to be filled. The divisions that follow competition and pride were described in the *Book of Mormon.*

> And now, in this two hundred and first year there began to be among them those who were lifted up in pride such as the wearing of costly apparel, and all manner of fine pearls, and of the fine things of the world.
>
> And from that time forth they did have their goods and their substance no more common among them.
>
> And they began to be divided into classes; and they began to build up churches unto themselves go get gain, and began to deny the true church of Christ. [4 Nephi 1:24–26]

Sometimes the proud are not all the way past feelings and they are led to reflect momentarily on the plight of the hungry. But Satan has an antidote for these momentary lapses into caring: blame the victims. After King Benjamin had instructed his people to succor and administer their substance to those in need, he warned:

> Perhaps thou shalt say: The man has brought upon himself his misery; therefore I will stay my hand, and will not give unto him of my food, nor impart unto him of my substance that he may not suffer, for his punishments are just.
>
> But I say unto you, O man, whosoever doeth this the same hath great cause to repent; and except he repenteth of that which he hath done he perisheth forever, and hath no interest in the kingdom of God.
>
> For behold, are we not all beggars? Do we not all depend upon

the same Being, even God, for all the substance which we have, for both food and raiment, and for gold, and for silver, and for all the riches which we have of every kind? [Mosiah 4:17–19]

The Alternative to Pride and Scarcity

The difference between the Savior's doctrine of abundance and the false principle of scarcity was illustrated in the desert of Judea. A multitude had followed the Savior to learn of Him but without taking thought of food. To feed this large gathering, Christ's disciples inventoried only five loaves and two fishes. Christ saw not the scarcity but the abundance, and fed the multitude of 5000. Afterwards, the disciples collected twelve baskets of surplus bread, which undoubtedly they used to serve other diners (Matthew 14:17–21).

The first recorded miracle of the Savior also emphasized the doctrine of abundance. At a wedding feast at which His mother had some responsibility, the wine was exhausted but not the capacity to create new wine. And the new wine that the Savior created was even better than what had been available before. The Savior proclaimed: "I am come that they might have life and that they might have it more abundantly" (John 10:10). To Joseph Smith the Lord revealed:

> For the earth is full, and there is enough and to spare; yea, I prepared all things and have given unto the children of men to be agents unto themselves.
>
> Therefore, if any man shall take of the abundance which I have made, and impart not his portion, according to the law of my gospel, unto the poor and the needy, he shall, with the wicked, lift up his eyes in hell, being in torment. [D&C 104:17–18]

I adapt a poem by Edwin Markham to illustrate the difference between the scarcity and competitive view of the world, and the abundance and sharing doctrine of the Savior:

> *[Pride] drew a circle that shut me out,*
> *heretic rebel a thing to flaunt,*

but love and I had the wit to win
[and] we drew a circle that took him in.

The Humble Who Believe in Abundance

The mission of the Church of Jesus Christ of Latter-day Saints is to bring souls to Christ. It is a mission of abundance in which all who are willing can achieve the prize of happiness, peace, and eternal life. Indeed, we are taught that the mission of the church is achieved by proclaiming the gospel, perfecting the saints, and redeeming the dead. But these three roads to the Savior are framed in abundance. Regarding our responsibility to our dead, Joseph Smith taught that their salvation is necessary and essential to our salvation—that they without us cannot be made perfect—neither can we without our dead be made perfect (D&C 128:15).

Regarding our responsibility to proclaim the gospel, the Lord revealed: "And if it so be that you should labor all your days in crying repentance unto this people, and bring save it be one soul unto me, how great shall be your joy with him in the kingdom of my Father!" (D&C 18:15). What an expansive and abundant view, that our joy is made full by giving our gospel light to others only to find our lights burn brighter. And finally, how is it that we progress toward perfection—having acquired all Christlike virtues? King Benjamin taught that when we are in the service of our fellow man we are in the service of our God and on the path toward perfection. For emphasis, the Savior taught that those who lose their lives for His sake shall find their lives perfected (Matthew 10:39).

Only the humble believe in abundance because only they recognize a power for creating abundance beyond their own. The humble do not limit their vision of the possible to what is on the table at any particular moment. Instead of focusing on the loaf, they pause before breaking bread to recognize the source of their daily bread, to acknowledge the power that created the seeds of grain and that allowed the earth and the elements to grow the grain, and to give thanks that

God gave them the strength to plant, harvest, thresh, and bake. They know their work was important. But the humble know that God made the harvest possible, and that if He desires He can bless them abundantly. Then, as the humble gather round the table, they are struck by the thought that without God's intervention, they would all be beggars. This common dependence on God and His mercies removes any artificial distinction that might otherwise separate them into groups competing for status.

The Lesson

We need to recognize that God created a world of abundance that requires cooperation to harvest and charity to share. If we cooperate and share and seek God's blessings, then we will all have enough and to spare. When the truth is known, we understand that there is more bread in the oven. Our peace and happiness require that we remember that it is the visit with our friend and not the car, the Kingdom of God and not worldly kingdoms, and the Savior not the Sabbath day that are the primary goods that bring peace and happiness.

Chapter Nine

9 – The Principle of Charity: The Pure Love of Christ

❧

The principle. Charity is the pure love of Christ (Moroni 7:47). The principle of charity confirms that: *if* you have charity, *then* you are filled with the desire to obey God and bless others. After Lehi tasted of the fruit of the tree of life, the love of Christ or charity, "[He] began to be desirous that [his] family should partake of it also" (1 Nephi 8:12). Enos when once filled with charity "began to feel a desire for the welfare of my brethren, the Nephites; wherefore, I did pour out my whole soul unto God for them" (Enos 1:9). After their being filled with charity, Alma and the sons of Mosiah "were desirous that salvation should be declared to every creature, for they could not bear that any human soul should perish; yea, even the very thoughts that any soul should endure endless torment did cause them to quake and tremble" (Mosiah 28:3). This same commitment to bless others is shown by all the prophet-leaders of the Book of Mormon.

Charity also moves us to keep the Lord's commandments. The Savior emphasized the connection between charity and commandment-keeping when He taught: "If ye love me, keep my commandments" (John 14:15). This scripture could be converted to the format of a principle, rendering the scripture: "*if* ye love me *then* you will keep my commandments."

Those who are filled with charity or the pure love of Christ have the remarkable ability to feel what others are feeling. Because of this unique ability, they are able to mourn with those that mourn, take joy in the success of others, and serve when assistance is needed.

Our two youngest sons taught me a great lesson on charity. All our sons wrestled. Despite all the coaching from his older brothers, our youngest son's first year in wrestling resulted in a perfect season—he lost every match. Between seasons, our boys worked together to help each other improve. Then came the first match of the next season and to our delight, at the end of the match Nathan had accumulated more points than his opponent. I happened to see Adam next to the mat with tears streaming down his cheeks. I was amazed. "What on earth is wrong?" I asked. "Nothing," he replied, "I'm just so happy to see Nathan do well that I can't help crying."

Moroni described the importance of charity and the means for obtaining it. He taught:

> But charity is the pure love of Christ, and it endureth forever; and whoso is found possessed of it at the last day, it shall be well with him.

> Wherefore, my beloved brethren, pray unto the Father with all the energy of heart, that ye may be filled with this love, which he hath bestowed upon all who are true followers of his Son, Jesus Christ. . . . [Moroni 7:47–48]

Bruce R. McConkie wrote of charity:

> Above all the attributes of godliness and perfection, charity is the one most devoutly to be desired. Charity is more than love, far more; it is everlasting love, perfect love, the pure love of Christ which endureth forever. It is love so centered in righteousness that the possessor has no aim or desire except for the eternal welfare of his own soul and for the souls of those around him.[1]

Alma the Elder taught that charity or the pure love of Christ is required for entrance into the church through the waters of baptism. Quoting Alma:

> And it came to pass that he said unto them: Behold, here are the waters of Mormon (for thus were they called) and now, as ye are desirous to come into the fold of God, and to be called his people, are willing to bear one another's burdens, that they may be light;
>
> Yea, and are willing to mourn with those that mourn; yea, and comfort those that stand in need of comfort, and to stand as witnesses of God at all times and in all things, and in all places that ye may be in. [Mosiah 18:8–9]

Alma described the true believer as one who could feel what others were feeling, and wanted the converts to understand that entrance into the kingdom of God required this ability or charity. Ammon and his brothers possessed this ability to feel for the well-being of others, the ability to walk in another's shoes. Of them we read: "Now they were desirous that salvation should be declared to every creature, for they could not bear that any human soul should perish; yea, even the very thought that any soul should endure endless torment did cause them to quake and tremble" (Mosiah 28:3). Sometimes popular performers come close to describing charity. For example, Barry Manilow sang: "you know that I'm sad when you're sad, and I'm glad when you're glad."

Filled with charity and the desire for the well-being of others, we naturally seek opportunities to serve. Neal A. Maxwell explained: "With increasing charity, then, our service to others will be an unforced thing [and] it will be a thing from inside, not from outside! Even the good we then do will be done for the right reasons and "not to please ourselves" (Romans 15:1).[2]

We may serve without charity and for selfish purposes, such as to be seen of man or to gain some material advantage. Service with a selfish intent is called priestcraft. However, those filled with charity cannot see another's need and not be moved to serve and share. Nephi taught his people about the difference between selfish service and charity motivated service. Referring to the Savior he taught:

He commandeth that there shall be no priestcrafts; for, behold, priestcrafts are that men preach and set themselves up for a light unto the world, that they may get gain and praise of the world; but they seek not for the welfare of Zion.

Behold, the Lord hath forbidden this thing; wherefore, the Lord God hath given a commandment that all men should have charity, which charity is love. And except they should have charity they were nothing. Wherefore, if they should have charity they would not suffer the laborer in Zion to perish. [2 Nephi 26:29–30]

How the Gift of Charity is Received

Bruce C. and Marie K. Hafen wrote eloquently of how charity is shared.

As we begin to follow Christ, then, the Lord gives us —a natural impulse to extend mercy and grace to others as we receive them from him. 'Because I have been given much,' we sing, 'I too must give.' As we reach our hands toward theirs, sometimes their reaching touches ours—and we somehow sense the Lord's grace coming back to us, multiplied, through them. As we receive God's love, we extend it to others in a circle that brings it back to us and brings us back to him. In this kind of life, a full life of *gracious* connections with other people, we live the spirit of charity.[3]

President Henry D. Moyle summarized one incident in our literature that describes how one person's reaching multiplied charity.[4]

Victor Hugo in his classic work *Les Miserables* describes a man named Jean Valjean who spends nineteen years as a prisoner in the galleys. His initial offense was stealing a loaf of bread to feed his mother's starving family. At that time he was only a boy. Upon his release from prison, after all others had rejected him as a despised ex-convict, he is finally befriended by a bishop, M. Beauvian.

This bishop treated Jean Valjean with great kindness and generosity. He trusted him and gave him food and lodging. Jean Valjean, unable to overcome the evil impulses fostered during his prison years, repaid the bishop by robbing him of his silverware, consisting of many priceless heirlooms. He was shortly after apprehended by the police and brought back, with the bishop's treasures in his bag. The bishop forgave Jean Valjean and, in place of accusing him of his dastardly deed of ingratitude, instantly said to him, "You forgot the candlesticks," and giving them to Jean Valjean, told him that they were silver, too. After the officers had left, the bishop said to the ex-convict: "Jean Valjean, my brother, you belong no longer to evil but to good . . . I will draw it [his soul] from dark thoughts and from the spirit of perdition"

This act of forgiveness on the part of a man whose property had been stolen aroused the latent virtues of Jean. They had lain dormant for nineteen years. Even his long term in the galleys could not destroy the inherent desire in man to do good. Almost his first act after the saintly deed of the bishop was to befriend a golden-haired girl in dire distress known as Cosette. The author's ultimate description of Jean Valjean is indicative of the tremendous transformation in the character of this unfortunate man. Cosette completed the reformation of this man's life which the bishop had initiated. Victor Hugo writes: "The Bishop had caused the dawn of virtue on his horizon; Cosette evoked the dawn of love."

After a life filled with charity, forgiveness and other good deeds, Jean Valjean sacrificed life itself for the happiness and well-being of Cosette and her husband. In his final letter to her, he wrote these words:

'I am writing just now to Cosette. She will find my letter. To her I bequeath the two candlesticks which are on the mantel. They are silver, but to me they are gold. They are diamonds. I do not know whether he who gave them to me is satisfied with me . . . I have done what I could."

There you have it. The charity of the Bishop filled Jean Valjean with charity that gave birth to service. Charity is the mother of Christian service. Perhaps this story helps us understand the scripture: "We love him [God] because he first loved us" (1 John 4:19). I believe that all of us could tell our own stories of how we learned about charity that would be similar to the story of Jean Valjean's, that because someone first loved us, we received the gift of charity that enabled us to love others.

Bonnie and I had been married only a few months when we moved from Logan, Utah where we both finished our undergraduate degrees, to Champaign/Urbana Illinois, where I was to begin my graduate studies at the University of Illinois. Our only income at the time was from my fellowship and occasionally some income Bonnie earned substitute teaching. In due time, Ryan, our first child was born, stretching even further our meager income. We reduced our budget in the only area that could be reduced—our food budget. We decided to eliminate one meal a day from our diet. As we attended church in what appeared to be an affluent ward, we sometimes wondered if we really belonged.

Then came Paul and Naomi Fitzgerald into out lives. Every Primary day (then held on a weekday) Naomi tended Ryan while Bonnie taught Primary and while I was at school. And always when we arrived to pick up Ryan, Paul and Naomi insisted we stay for dinner. Their home was a little piece of heaven for us, a place where kind and caring people expressed a concern for our well being, lifted our spirits, and provided welcome nourishment. Somehow we felt like we had been adopted into their family. We can never repay Paul and Naomi for their kindness that came at a time when we most needed charity.

Years later I learned about the ripple effect of charity when one time I had the privilege of introducing my mother to Naomi Fitzgerald. My mother told Naomi something I shall never forget. Mother said to Naomi: "The nicest thing you can do for a mother is to be kind to her children. Thank you." It was at that moment that I gained some insight into King Benjamin's instruction that we serve God best by serving his children (Mosiah 2:17). I suppose that the nicest thing we can do for our Heavenly Father is to love and serve His children.

Charity and its Companions, Faith and Hope

Moroni described charity as keeping company with hope and faith. Yet charity, he wrote, is the greatest of all the gifts of God. The reason that it is the greatest gift of God is that it is impossible to have faith in God and the divine mission of Jesus Christ unless we have charity. The connection between hope, faith, and charity is clear upon reflection. We cannot hope that the Savior suffered our pains and those of all mankind and that He gained the victory over death unless we can believe that He loves us, for only love could motivate such a sacrifice. And we cannot have the faith that leads from belief to duty unless we have experienced at least a taste of charity that would lead Christ to the infinite sacrifice. When we ourselves feel pure love, then it is much easier to have faith in and hope that Christ also has this pure love for us. Nephi noted that he did not require the knowledge of all things as long as he knew that God loved him: "I know that he loveth his children; nevertheless, I do not know the meaning of all things" (1 Nephi 11:17).

We observe that those filled with faith, hope, and charity are fearless. What a transformation occurred in Peter between the time of his fearful denial of friendship with the Savior in front of street merchants to his bold declaration before Annas and Caiaphas and other rulers. To the rulers who asked by what authority were his miracles performed, he declared:

> Be it known unto you all, and to all the people of Israel, that by the name of Jesus Christ of Nazareth, whom ye crucified, whom God raised from the dead, even by him doth this man stand here before you whole.
>
> This is the stone which was set at naught of you builders, which is become the head of the corner.
>
> Neither is there salvation in any other: for there is none other name

under heaven given among men, whereby we must be saved. [Acts 4:10–12]

Peter's temerity had been replaced by charity induced boldness. Similarly, those filled with charity fear only committing sin which would separate them from the love of Christ.

Charity also has the capacity to deflate puffed up egos. Since we know that the love of God and His power sustain us, we take no credit for our successes except to acknowledge the receipt of His gifts and commit ourselves to use them in His service. Thus, charity most frequently walks with humility.

Finally, charity prevents burnout. Elder F. Enzio Busche of the Seventy once attended our stake conference. I asked him how to deal with burnout in church service. He answered that laboring without charity is exhausting. Laboring because one possesses charity is renewing. Does a mother's love for her children ever die? Does the mother say, "I just need to be released for a few months or a couple of years so I can have a little time for myself?" Elder Busche remarked, that there is no shortage of spiritual energy in the kingdom of Heavenly Father when the souls of the Saints are filled with charity.

> And charity suffereth long, and is kind, and envieth not, and is not puffed up, seeketh not her own, is not easily provoked, thinketh no evil, and rejoiceth not in iniquity but rejoiceth in the truth, beareth all things, believeth all things, hopeth all things, endureth all things.
>
> Wherefore, my beloved brethren, if ye have not charity, ye are nothing, for charity never faileth. Wherefore, cleave unto charity, which is the greatest of all the gifts of God, for all things must fail— [Moroni 7:45–46]

The Lesson

The Atonement of Jesus Christ was the greatest act of charity that has ever been performed. His Atonement that required an infinite personal sacrifice could only have been motivated by a power equal to the awfulness of the pain, the power of charity. Only charity has the power to move us to offer all that we have. Charity is not only the greater motivator, it is also the greatest benefactor bringing to those who enjoy it, supreme joy and happiness. Satisfaction derived from another source can never compare with the supernal joy and happiness associated with charity. Writing about God's gift of charity to each of us who desire it, Nephi declared:

> And the angel said unto me: Behold the Lamb of God, yea, even the Son of the Eternal Father! Knowest thou the meaning of the tree which thy father saw?
>
> And I answered him, saying: Yea, it is the love of God, which sheddeth itself abroad in the hearts of the children of men; wherefore, it is the most desirable above all things.
>
> And he spake unto me, saying: Yea, and the most joyous to the soul. [1 Nephi 11:21–23]

Chapter Ten

10 – Principle of At-one-ment: After All that We Can Do

ༀ

The principle. The principle of at-one-ment declares that *because* of the Atonement of Jesus Christ, *[then]* all mankind may be saved by obedience to the laws and ordinances of the gospel.[1] Jacob taught the principle of at-one-ment to the Nephites. "It has been made manifest unto me, for I have heard and seen; and it also has been made manifest unto me by the power of the Holy Ghost; wherefore, I know if there should be no atonement made all mankind must be lost" (Jacob 7:12). Abinadi taught the principle of at-one-ment to the wicked king Noah and his priests. "Were it not for the atonement, which God himself shall make for the sins and iniquities of his people . . . they must unavoidably perish" (Mosiah 13:28).

What the atonement of Jesus Christ and our obedience save us from are separations and sorrows. What Christ's atonement saves us for are at-one-ments and joy. Jacob described the separations the Christ's Atonement saves us from when he wrote: "O how great the goodness of our God, who prepareth a way for our escape from the grasp of this awful monster; yea, that monster, death [the separation of the body and the spirit] and hell [the separation of man from the presence of God], which I call the death of the body, and also the death of the spirit" (2 Nephi 9:10–11). Nephi, a prophet descended from Lehi and Nephi, described the at-one-ments and joy that the Atonement saves us for. These existed among the people in the Americas following Christ's visit.

> And there were no envyings, nor strifes, nor tumults, nor whoredoms, nor lyings, nor murders, nor any manner of lasciviousness; and surely there could not be a *happier people* among all the people who had been created by the hand of God.
>
> There were no robbers, nor murderers, neither were there Lamanites, nor any manner of -ites; but *they were in one*, the children of Christ, and heirs to the kingdom of God. [4 Nephi 1:16–17; italics added]

Because the atonement of Jesus Christ saves us from separations and sorrows and saves us for at-one-ment and joy, it is the most important event that ever has or will occur. Speaking about the importance of Christ's atonement, Elder Bruce R. McConkie taught: "The Atonement is the most transcendent doctrine of the Gospel. It is the most important single thing that has ever occurred in the history of the world, or ever will occur. It is the foundation upon which all other things rest. If it weren't for the Atonement, we could write the Gospel off as a myth and the whole purpose of the creation would be frustrated.[2]

Joseph Smith placed the Atonement of Jesus Christ at the center of the gospel when he taught: "the fundamental principles of our religion are the testimony of the Apostles and Prophets, concerning Jesus Christ, that He died, was buried, and rose again the third day, and ascended into heaven; and all other things which pertain to our religion are only appendages to it."[3]

Separations and the Need for At-one-ment

I believe that separations produce most of our sorrows. I expect that we all have our own stories to tell about painful separations. I recall the day I left home to begin my college education. I don't remember the reason, but I recall with sorrow, that before I left, my mother and I had a disagreement. I know I said something that hurt her feelings and as a result, she did not accompany my father and me to Logan Utah where I began my freshman year at Utah State University. I also remember my first few days in Logan, separated from my family and most of my friends. In those first days away from home I experienced a painful loneliness because of the emotional distance that existed between my mother and me and the physical distance that separated me from my family.

Another separation that is seared into my soul occurred many years later. I had completed a mission, graduated from Utah State, married my sweetheart, Bonnie, was the father of our first child, and was attending graduate school in Champaign/Urbana, Illinois. An opportunity came for Bonnie and me to return home to Fillmore, Utah for a visit and to introduce our son to his grandparents. We had a wonderful visit and then, all too soon, it was time to leave. Dad and Mom accompanied us to the car to say good-bye. I had a feeling come over me that this was the last time I would see my father alive. It was an overpowering feeling of sadness because I had depended on him throughout all my life for counsel and support. Besides Bonnie, he and Mom were my best friends and the thought that we would be separated was depressing. Dad may have also felt the coming separation, because for the first time that I can ever remember, he had tears in his eyes. A few short months later we received the phone call telling us that Dad had died of a sudden heart attack.

Now many years later, Bonnie and I are facing other kinds of separation. We are living the separation from our youth and find it more difficult to jog our favorite five mile route around Okemos Square. We have also experienced separations from our children. As of this writing, we have watched them leave for missions and school and to begin their own homes. We are coming to appreciate just a little of what Heavenly Father must experience when each of His children leaves His heavenly home for their mortal education.

But none of the separations described thus far inflict the pain I have felt on occasion and watched others experience as a result of sin. Sin separates us from the presence of the Lord and the influence of the Holy Ghost. Sin not only pains the sinner but also afflicts those who love the sinner. I once held a dear brother in my arms as he wept over his son's transgression that disqualified him from serving a mission and led to the birth of a child for which neither the father nor the mother were prepared. I have watched the ripple effects of sin created by a father's extramarital affair that broke his wife's heart and destroyed the confidence of his children. I have participated in the pain created by a child who separated herself from self-control and traded agency for an addiction to harmful drugs. From all these experiences and more, I conclude that our most painful separation is between our sin stained souls and God.

The Good News

At the beginning of my calling to serve as the president of the Lansing, Michigan stake, my counselors and I wrote a statement of purpose that we hoped would guide our efforts. The introduction to that statement of purpose read:

> The essence of the Gospel is the Atonement of Jesus Christ. As we come to see the importance of the Atonement, we must also see the need to live the principles of the Gospel; because only by living the principles of the Gospel can we receive all of the blessings it makes possible. These blessings include being one with the Father and the Son, with our Christlike selves, and with others.[4]

We hoped that our statement of purpose would communicate the good news that through the Atonement of Christ all mankind may be saved from the separations that limit our joy and restrict our progress.

Overcoming Separations

The principle of restoration declares that which we send out will be restored. The principle of at-one-ment declares that what is to be restored is at-one-ment or separation depending on our choices. Thus, all principles point to Christ's atonement on which at-one-ment depends. This focus on Christ's future Atonement led the Book of Mormon prophet Amulek to write: "And behold, this is the whole meaning of the law, every whit pointing to that great and last sacrifice; and that great and last sacrifice will be the Son of God, yea, infinite and eternal" (Alma 34:14). While the laws of Moses directed attention forward to the Atonement, gospel principles taught today call our attention back to the keystone event in world history, the Atonement of Jesus Christ.

The gospel greets us with the good news that the separation of man's physical body from his spirit has been overcome by Christ's resurrection. It also trumpets the good news that our painful separations from God's spirit and a clear conscience have been overcome by Christ's Atonement on condition that we repent and govern ourselves by correct principles. "And he cometh into the world that he may save all men if they will hearken unto his voice" (2 Nephi 9:21).

The Savior's Atonement opened the door to the possibility of at-one-ment between man and God. It was the greatest event ever to occur. It was the climax of Christ's earthly ministry, the apex of devotion and love. Because of Christ's Atonement, all men will be resurrected and have their bodies and spirits reunited. The resurrection is a free gift to all. As in Adam all die, even so in Christ shall all be made alive (1 Corinthians 15:22). In addition, overcoming the separation between man and God, the spiritual death, because of Christ's Atonement is now a possibility if we are willing (Hebrews 9:12; Moroni 10:33).

"All That We Can Do"

Becoming one with our Savior and our Father in Heaven, with our better selves, and with our brothers and sisters, what Christ prayed for in the Garden of Gethsemane, requires not only His Atonement, but also all that we can do. The balance between the Savior's grace and our best effort was summarized by Nephi. He wrote: "For we labor diligently to write, to persuade our children, and also our brethren, to believe in Christ, and to be reconciled to God; for we know that it is by grace that we are saved, after all we can do" (2 Nephi 25:23). Some of those things that we can do to achieve at-one-ment are described next.

Be one with the Savior by letting His will be our own. In the crucible of Gethsemane, Christ asked: "if it be possible let this cup pass from me." Then he yielded His will to that of His Father with his declaration: "not my will, but thine, be done" (Luke 22:42). Thus, the will of Father became the will of the Savior. His unity with his Father led Christ to declare: "I and my Father are one" (John 10:30). We become one with the Savior when His will becomes our will. Like the Savior, we must be willing to declare, "not my will, but thine, be done."

Be one with the Savior by following His example. As Christ's disciples, we should follow Christ's example just as He followed the example of His Father. Christ declared: "The Son can do nothing of himself, but what he seeth the Father do" (John 5:19). Christ's commitment to follow the example of His Father led Him to teach Philip: "He that hath seen me hath seen the Father" (John 14:9). We become one with the Savior when His life becomes the pattern for our own lives.

Be one with the Savior by becoming one with others. We become one with the Savior by loving those He loves, all of God's children. We express this love by sharing the gospel with our non-member friends and family and by opening the door to gospel opportunities for the deceased by performing sacred temple ordinances for the dead.

At-one-ment with others is a natural result of being one with the Savior and with our Christlike selves. King Benjamin noted that once we have personally tasted of the goodness of God and retained a remission of our sins, we will not have a mind to injure one another and we will render to every man that which is due. In addition, we will provide for our children and teach them to obey the laws of God and refrain from fighting and quarrelling. Finally, once we have tasted of the goodness of God, we will love and serve others (Mosiah 4:13–15).

Our desire to serve others and to lead them to the joy that we feel is always a natural desire for those who partake of the sweet peace the gospel brings to those who practice correct principles. After he partook of the fruit of the tree of life, the prophet Lehi desired that his family might also partake (see 1 Nephi 8:12). The importance of sharing the fruit of the tree of life with others is taught by the Lord in blessings given to John and Peter Whitmer. "And now, behold, I say unto you, that the thing which will be of the most worth unto you will be to declare repentance unto this people, that you may bring souls unto me, that you may rest with them in the kingdom of my Father" (D&C 15:6, 16:6). Sharing the gospel is important even for those who are dead, for we cannot be made perfect or happy without them.

Be one with the Savior by doing for others what we ask Heavenly Father to do for us. We approach our Christlike selves when we do for others what we ask Heavenly Father to do for us. The golden rule directs us to do for others what we wish they would do for us. The *celestial rule* directs us to do for others what we ask God to do for us. We pray for forgiveness. Christ asks us to forgive those who have trespassed against us. We pray for comfort when we mourn. Christ asks us to mourn with those who need comfort. We pray for help in achieving our worthy goals. Christ asks us to find joy in the success of others. We pray for freedom and the right to choose. Christ asks us to respect the agency of others and never force the human soul. We pray that our burdens may be light. Christ asks us to lighten the loads of others. We pray that we may one day return to the presence of our Heavenly Father. Christ asks us to open up our homes for His children. If we will do for one another what we pray that the Father will do for us, He will with gratitude declare: inasmuch as ye have done it unto one of the least of these my brethren, ye have done it unto me (Matthew 25:40).

Be one with the Savior by entering into sacred two-way promises with Him called covenants. At the sacrament table we promise to take upon ourselves the name of Christ, to always remember Him, and to keep His commandments. He covenants that if we keep our promises, He will bless us with His Spirit. When we enjoy the companionship of His spirit, we approach at-one-ment with Him because we are of the same spirit. But the way to "at-one-ment," to the companionship of the Lord's spirit, is through the keeping of covenants. Other covenants, including those associated with the priesthood and the temple, reflect our growing commitment to the Savior.

Our growing commitments to the Savior reflected by our covenants may be likened to those commitments made by young couples. Their commitment begins with an interest in each other's activity and results in casual dating. Then as their interests in each other increase, the importance of other relationships decreases. Finally, when the relationship has grown to maturity so that confidence in each other's commitment is complete, then a two-way covenant of marriage makes two into one. Small wonder then, that when describing our relationship to Him, He described Himself as the bridegroom and the church as the bride.

Be one with the Savior by remembering His Atonement. My mother told me that when I was born, my father wanted to name me after a member of his family, but that she didn't like the name. So she encouraged him to give me his first name. I'm glad he did. I have been honored to carry his name and it has the added benefit of causing me to remember him, especially when I write my name or hear it spoken. Helaman named his sons Lehi and Nephi so they would remember their noble ancestors and seek to pattern their lives after them (see Helaman 5:6). So likewise when we pray, when we sing hymns, when we partake of the sacrament, when we read the scriptures, or when we see a beautiful sunset, we remember our Savior and our Father in Heaven and we feel a sense of being one.

At the conclusion of his sermon, King Benjamin taught the importance of remembering: But this much I can tell you, that if ye do not watch yourselves, and your thoughts, and your words, and your deeds, and observe the commandments of God, and continue in the faith of what ye have heard concerning the coming of our Lord, even unto the end of hour lives, ye must perish. *And now O man, remember, and perish not* (Mosiah 4:30; italics added).

Be one with the Savior by practicing the first principles and ordinances of the gospel. The Savior taught the Nephites that the gospel is that He came to do the will of the Father and to work out the Atonement (3 Nephi 27). It follows that the first principles and ordinances of the gospel are also the first principles and ordinances of the Atonement. These principles and ordinances are designed to overcome our separation from God and our better selves. The first principles focus on faith and hope in him and his redeeming atonement. Next they require that we repent by turning away from sin to the commandments of God. Then that direct us to the ordinances of baptism and the confirmation of the Holy Ghost. These first principles and ordinances involve the grace of the Savior and all that we can do. The Savior taught the first principles and ordinances of the Atonement using the following words:

> And it shall come to pass, that whoso repenteth and is baptized in my name shall be filled; and if he endureth to the end, behold, him will I hold guiltless before my father at that day when I shall stand to judge the world . . .

> Now this is the commandment: Repent, all ye ends of the earth, and come unto me and be baptized in my name, that ye may be sanctified by the reception of the Holy Ghost, that ye may stand spotless before me at the last day. [3 Nephi 27:16, 20]

The first principles and ordinances are what we do to formally accept the blessings of Christ's Atonement. We become one with Him by cleansing ourselves through repentance; by growing in our faith in His power to rescue us from sin; by making covenants with Him through the ordinance of baptism; and by receiving His gift of the Holy Ghost.

A Symbol of Christ's Atonement

Atonement means to set at one those who have been estranged and denotes the reconciliation of God to man.[5] The scriptures instruct us that one symbol of Christ's Atonement is an embrace. "The Lord hath redeemed my soul from hell; I have beheld his glory, and I am encircled about eternally in the arms of his love" (2 Nephi 1:15). And: "O Lord, wilt thou encircle me around in the robe of thy righteousness?" (2 Nephi 4:33). "Behold, he sendeth an invitation unto all men, for the arms of mercy are extended towards them, and he saith: Repent, and I will receive you" (Alma 5:33).

An atonement is described in the parable of the prodigal son whose reconciliation with father is symbolized with an embrace (Luke 15:11–32). The son had humbled himself and agreed in his own heart to be his father's servant. Feeling his son's contrition and righteous desires, the father embraced and forgave his son all his wrongs. The embrace signaled the atonement of the prodigal son and his father. Clearly it was an unequal sacrifice that led to an at-one-ment between the prodigal son and his farther. And so it will be with us in our at-one-ment with our Father in Heaven.

The application of the prodigal son parable is obvious. We have been given a rich inheritance that we squander when we sin. Feeling remorse for the misuse of our inheritance leads us to repentance and to turn toward our Heavenly home. Then our Father in Heaven, recognizing our contrition and righteous desires, welcomes us home with an embrace.

The Lesson

Man is that he might have joy. Our joy is the object and design of the gospel. It is promised to all of us who embrace Christ's Atonement and become one with Him, our Christlike selves, and others with similar desires. These at-one-ments are achieved by learning and practicing correct principles. The gospel of Jesus Christ teaches correct principles. We practice them as we serve our brothers and sisters. This service will likely begin with our friends and family. Then, like Enos, our desires to be one will extend to those who consider us to be their enemies. At some point our at-one-ment efforts will extend to those on the other side of the veil and we will work to redeem the dead.

All of these opportunities to be one lead us to proclaim the gospel message of joy recorded by the Prophet Joseph Smith: "Now, what do we hear in the gospel which we have received? A voice of gladness! A voice of mercy from heaven; and a voice of truth out of the earth; glad tidings for the dead; a voice of gladness for the living and the dead; glad tidings of great joy. How beautiful upon the mountains are the feet of those that bring glad tidings of good things, and that say unto Zion; Behold, thy God reigneth! (D&C 128:19).

On June 27, 1844 Joseph Smith and his brother Hyrum were martyred in Carthage, Illinois. The enemies of the church believed that with his death "Mormonism" would end. But it did not end. In the April 1997 General Conference of the church, five quorums of the Seventy were organized to administer to a church membership of millions located in nearly all parts of the world. The principles for organizing the additional quorums of Seventy were described in a revelation received by Joseph Smith on March 28, 1835 (D&C

107:94–97) and provide directions for maintaining unity in the worldwide church today.

Besides teaching the organizational structure needed to sustain the Church from its birth to its world wide reach, the Prophet Joseph Smith taught correct principles needed to administer welfare programs, temple and genealogy work, and missionary work. He also taught the pre-eminence of the family, principles of health and education, and succession in the presidency of the Church. The great work that Joseph Smith began and that modern prophets continue did not end with his martyrdom in Carthage, nor in Council Bluffs after the Saints were forced to flee their homes in Nauvoo. The great work did not end because those who followed after Joseph Smith continued to teach and to be governed by correct principles.

Epilogue

❦

Elder Dallin H. Oaks once asked a member of the Quorum of the Twelve to review a talk he had written. His colleague and companion in the quorum returned the talk with the review comment: "Therefore what?"[1] Therefore what? is an appropriate question that should be asked of any written work, including this one. My answer to "Therefore what?" follows.

In a most insightful summary of human needs, a subject of intellectual discussions across the ages, President Gordon B. Hinckley taught: "Every new member [and all of the rest of us] needs three things: a friend, a meaningful assignment, and to be nurtured by the good word of God."[2] If we were to add to President Hinckley's list the need for bread, we would summarize in a few words a great deal of what has been written about human behavior and its motivation.

Needs, or conditions requiring relief, direct our desires, organize our resources, and move us to act. How we respond to our needs makes all the difference. Our needs may lead us to destruction, as in the case of King David and Bathsheba, or inspire us to distinguished service, as in the case of Helaman's stripling warriors. They can lead us to unnecessary engine replacements or to invest in temples as did the early saints in Kirtland and Nauvoo.[3]

The difference between essential temple investments and unnecessary engine replacements is often an understanding of correct principles. The Lord declared that: many "are kept from the truth because they know not where to find it—" (D&C 123:12). Lehi recognized the need for the correct principles contained in the sacred writings of the prophets, and sent his sons to retrieve them. The Savior reminded the Nephites of the need for correct principles and reproved them for not writing the words of the prophets. In our own time we have been commanded to keep journals so that we may remember the lessons we have learned in our search for correct principles.

Correct principles, designed for our happiness, do so only when applied. Correct principles are like a banquet of nutrition and delicious food that only tickles our senses unless consumed and internalized. Correct principles are like power tools that only are valuable when used. Carrying correct principles from the classroom to our various work stations in the kingdom and there laboring with all our might to become one is the "therefore what?" of this and any other work with a similar purpose. Otherwise, we are like the turkeys who attended flying classes where they soared like eagles and, after the classes were over, walked home.[4] If we have been taught correct principles and fail to apply them, then we are like a man beholding his natural face in a glass "and who after seeing himself in the glass goes his way and forgets what manner of man he was" (James 1:23, 24). My testimony is that the gospel of Jesus Christ teaches true principles which will bring us joy if we use them to govern our lives.

Endnotes

❦

Introduction

[1] Quoted by John Taylor, *Millennial Star* (15, November 1851) 339.

Preface – Principles

[1] Boyd K. Packer, "The Word of Wisdom: The Principle and the Promise," *Ensign* (May 1996), 17.

[2] John B. Dickson, "A Brief Introduction to the Church," *Ensign* (May 2000), 82.

[3] In Hebraic writing, *if A then B* might be written as *if A and B*. Thus in many principles with a promise the word *then* is implied. For a discussion on this point see Royal Skousen, "How Joseph Smith Translated the Book of Mormon: Evidence from the Original Manuscript," *Journal of Book of Mormon Studies,* Volume 7, Number 1 (1998) 28.

[4] Harold B. Lee, "Admonitions for the Priesthood of God," *Ensign* (January 1973) 104.

[5] Dallin H. Oaks, "Revelation." *New Era* (September 1982) 38.

[6] I have been unable to remember or discover the source of this story.

[7] Phillip K. Howard, *The Death of Common Sense: How Law Is Suffocating America*, Random House, 1994.

Chapter 1

[1] Ralph Waldo Emerson, quoted by Marvin J. Ashton in "What Is a Friend?" *Ensign* (January 1973) 41.

[2] Paul G. Hewitt, *"Points to Ponder," Reader's Digest* (April 1993) 35.

[3] Quoted in *Favorite Quotations from the Collection of Thomas S. Monson.* (1985) 150.

[4] Dorothy Law Nolte, "Children Live What They Learn," quoted by Neil J. Flinders in "Principles of Parenting, Part 2," *Ensign* (April 1975) 50.

Chapter 2

[1] John A. Widtsoe, "The Two Factors of Happiness," in *Handbook of the Restoration: A Selection of Gospel Themes Discussed by Various Authors,* Independence, Mo.: Zion's Printing and Publishing Co., 1944, pp. 177–269.

[2] Robert Frost, "The Road Not Taken," *Book of Poetry of Robert Frost,* edited by Edward Connery Lathem, New York, Holt Brineholt, and Winston, 1974, p. 105.

[3] Letter from Christie Howes, February 25, 1998, quoted by Neal A. Maxwell, "Repent of [Our] Selfishness," *Ensign* (May 1999) 25.

[4] Sterling W. Sill. *BYU Speeches of the Year/1962*, (February 21, 1962) 6.

[5] Stephen E. Robinson. *Following Christ: The parable of the diver and other good news.* Deseret Book Company, Salt Lake City, 1995, p. 57.

[6] Quoted by James E. Faust, "The Power of Self-Mastery." *Ensign* (May 2000) 43.

[7] Bill Russell and Taylor Branch, *Second Wind*, New York: Random House, 1979, p. 155.

[8] Spencer W. Kimball, *Faith Precedes the Miracle,* Deseret Book Company, Salt Lake City, Utah, 1974, p. 99.

[9] Richard G. Scott, "Trust in the Lord," *Ensign* (November 1995) 16.

[10] Albert Ellis described one of three great lies to be: "life should be easy." Ellis, Albert and Robert Harper. *Guide to Rational Living.* Englewood Cliff N.J.: Prentice-Hall, 1961.

[11] Eliza R. Snow. "Think not, When You Gather to Zion." *Hymns: The Church of Jesus Christ of Latter-day Saints*, Deseret Book Company, Salt Lake City, Utah, 31st printing, 1973, Hymn 21.

[12] Tom Gantert, "Mentor's Senses are Sharp," *Lansing State Journal*, Tuesday, January 27, 1998, pp. 4a, 4c.

Chapter 3

[1] Ezra Taft Benson, *Teachings of Ezra Taft Benson*, Bookcraft, Salt Lake City, Utah, 1988, p.8.

[2] Spencer J. Condie. *In Perfect Balance,* Bookcraft, Salt Lake City, 1993.

[3] Boyd K. Packer, "The Only True and Living Church," *Ensign* (December 1971) 40–42.

[4] Dallin H. Oaks, "Our Strengths Can Become Our Downfall," *Ensign* (October, 1994) 11.

[5] L. Tom Perry, "Called of God," *Ensign* (November 2002) 7.

[6] Gordon B. Hinckley, "Our Fading Civility," BYU commencement address, 25 Apr. 1996, p. 15. Quoted by Joseph B. Wirthlin in "Lessons Learned in the Journey of Life," *Ensign,* (December 2000) 10.

Chapter 4

[1] Patricia Skalka, "How to Mend a Broken Friendship," *Readers Digest* (June 1999) 40.

[2] James E. Talmage, *The Vitality of Mormonism: Brief Essay on the Distinctive Doctrines of the Church of Jesus Christ of Latter-day Saints*, Richard G. Badger: Boston, 1919, p. 262.

[3] Ezra Taft Benson, *Children's Friend* (April 1957) 26. Quoted by Gordon B. Hinckley, "This Work Will Go Forward," *Ensign* (November 1990) 4, 5.

[4] Lindon J. Robison, *Becoming A Zion People*, Hawkes Publishing Inc., 1992, p. 72.

Chapter 5

[1] Gordon B. Hinckley, Heber City/Springville, Utah, regional conference, priesthood leadership meeting, May 13, 1995, quoted by Earl C. Tingey, "Keeping the Sabbath Day Holy," *Ensign* (February 2000) 49.

[2] Peter McGrath. "The Battle of Britain, 50 Years Ago." *Newsweek* (August 20, 1990) 56.

[3] Spencer W. Kimball, *Miracle of Forgiveness*, Bookcraft: Salt Lake City, Utah, 1969, p. 240.

[4] Bruce R. McConkie, *Mormon Doctrine 2nd edition,* Bookcraft, Salt Lake City, 1979, p. 848.

[5] Robert Rosenthal and Lenore Jacobson, *Pygmalion in the Classroom: Teacher Expectation and Pupil Intellectual Development.* New York: Holt, Rinehart and Winston, Inc., 1968.

[6] Boyd K. Packer, "The Unwritten Order of Things." Brigham Young University 1996–97 Speeches, October 15, 1996, p. 7, 8.

[7] *Gospel Doctrine: Selections from the Sermons and Writings of Joseph F. Smith.* 6th ed. Deseret Book Company: Salt Lake City Utah, 1943, p. 14.

[8] William Shakespeare. *Hamlet.* (Act 1, sc. 3).

[9] Joseph Fielding Smith compiler, *Teachings of the Prophet Joseph Smith,* Deseret News Press: Salt Lake City, 1976, p. 151.

[10] Boyd K. Packer, "Personal Revelation: The Gift, the Test, and the Promise," *Ensign* (November 1994) 59.

[11] David O. McKay, "Cleanliness Is Next to Godliness," *Instructor* (March 1965) 86.

[12] David O. McKay. *Conference Report, October 1967,* p. 96.

[13] Richard L. Evans, "One Small Step." *Improvement Era* (June 1970) 38.

[14] Alexander Pope, "An Essay on Man," Epistle 2, lines 217ff.

[15] C. S. Lewis, *Mere Christianity*. New York: Macmillan, 1952, pp. 53, 54.

Chapter 6

[1] Neal A. Maxwell. "Becometh As a Child." *Ensign* (May 1996) 68.

[2] Parley P. Pratt, *Autobiography of Parley Parker Pratt*. Edited by his son Parley P. Pratt. 6th Edition. Deseret Book Company, Salt Lake City Utah, 1964, p. 211.

Chapter 7

[1] Bruce R. McConkie. *The Promised Messiah: The first coming of Christ*. Deseret Book Company, Salt Lake City, 1981, p. xvii.

[2] Neal A. Maxwell, "Meekness—A Dimension of True Discipleship." *Ensign* (March 1983) 70.

[3] Sheri Dew, *Biography of Gordon B. Hinckley*, Deseret Book Company: Salt Lake City, Utah, 1998.

[4] Daniel K. Judd. "'Not As the World Giveth. . .' : Mormonism and Popular Psychology," in *'To Be Learned Is Good If . . . '* edited by Robert L. Millet, Bookcraft: Salt Lake City, 1987, p. 149.

[5] Bruce R. McConkie, "The Dead Who Die in the Lord" *Ensign* (November 1976) 106.

[6] Ezra Taft Benson, "Jesus Christ—Gifts and Expectations," *New Era* (May 1975) 16–21.

[7] Martin Luther, "A Mighty Fortress Is Our God," *Hymns of the Church of Jesus Christ of Latter-day Saints*, 1985, hymn no. 68.

Chapter 8

[1] Adam Smith. *The Wealth of Nations*. (First Published, 1776). Chicago: Henry Regnery Co., 1966, p. 25.

[2] Nauvoo's economy prior to the exodus was characterized by an impressive number of trades and occupations that contributed to its economic success; cf. James A. Warner and Styne M. Slade, *The Mormon Way,* Englewood Cliffs, NJ: Prentice-Hall, 1976, p. 15.

[3] Amartya Sen, *Development As Freedom,* Alfred A. Knopf, New York, 1999, p. 16.

[4] Ezra Taft Benson, "Beware of Pride," *Ensign* (May 1989) 4.

[5] C. S. Lewis, *Mere Christianity*, New York: Macmillan, 1952, pp. 109–110.

[6] Hugh Nibley refers to primary and secondary goods as goods of first and second intent. See Hugh Nibley, "Goods of First and Second Intent," in *Approaching Zion*, edited by Don E. Norton, Deseret Book Company: Salt Lake City and Foundation for Ancient Research and Mormon Studies, Provo, Utah, 1989, pp. 524–553.

[7] John A. Widtsoe compiler, *Discourses of Brigham Young,* Deseret Book Company: Salt Lake City, Utah, 1951 edition, p. 307.

[8] Quoted in: "Gospel of Love: Stories About Spencer W. Kimball," *Ensign* (December 1985) 20.

Chapter 9

[1] Bruce R. McConkie, *Mormon Doctrine.* 2nd ed. Salt Lake City: Bookcraft, 1966, p. 121.

[2] Neal A. Maxwell, *Notwithstanding my Weakness*, Deseret Book: Salt Lake City, 1981, p. 29.

[3] Bruce C. and Marie K. Hafen, *The Belonging Heart: The Atonement and Relationships with God and Family,* Deseret Book Company: Salt Lake City, 1994, p. 17.

[4] Henry D. Moyle, "As We Forgive." *Improvement Era* (November 1957) 814, 815.

Chapter 10

[1] The Articles of Faith of the Church of Jesus Christ of Latter-day Saints, Article 3.

[2] Bruce R. McConkie, *The Atonement*, Brigham Young University Speeches of the Year, 6 May 1953, p.1.

[3] Joseph Fielding Smith compiler, *Teachings of the Prophet Joseph Smith*, Deseret News Press: Salt Lake City, 1976, p. 121.

[4] Mission Statement for the Lansing Michigan stake, copyright 1994 and published by the Lansing Michigan Stake of the Church of Jesus Christ of Latter-day Saints 431 East Saginaw, East Lansing, MI, 48823.

[5] *Bible Dictionary*, published by the Church of Jesus Christ of Latter-day Saints, Salt Lake City, Utah, 1989, p. 617.

Epilogue

[1] Dallin H. Oaks, "Following the Pioneers," *Ensign* (November 1997) 72.

[2] Gordon B. Hinckley, "Converts and Young Men." *Ensign* (May 1997) 47.

[3] Karl Ricks Anderson, *Joseph Smith's Kirtland: Eyewitness Accounts*, Deseret Book Company, Salt Lake City, Utah, 1989, pp. 15–16.

[4] Merlin R. Lybbert, "A Latter-day Samaritan" *Ensign* (May 1990) 82.

About the Author

❦

Lindon J. Robison and his wife, Bonnie, are the parents of five children and live in Okemos, Michigan where he is a professor of agricultural economics at Michigan State University. Some of the materials presented in this book are drawn from talks he gave while serving as the stake president of the Lansing Michigan stake.

Brother Robison holds a B.S. degree from Utah State University, an M.S. degree from the University of Illinois, a Ph.D. from Texas A&M University and did post graduate work at George Washington University. He has been a visiting professor at the University of Minnesota (St. Paul), Brigham Young University, and the Swedish University of Agricultural Sciences. He is the author of numerous articles, bulletins, book chapters and books, including *Becoming A Zion People*.

Brother Robison has served as a bishop, a stake president, an area authority in the North America Northeast area, and currently serves as president of the Spain, Malaga mission.